THE LEAP

THE LEAP

Are You Ready to Live a New Reality?

CONSTANCE KELLOUGH

NAMASTE PUBLISHING
VANCOUVER, CANADA

Library and Archives Canada Cataloguing in Publication

Kellough, Constance, 1947–
The leap : are you ready to live a new reality? / Constance Kellough.

Includes bibliographical references.
ISBN 978-1-897238-27-1

1. Spiritual life. 2. Consciousness—Religious aspects. 3. Quietude.
4. Self-realization—Religious aspects. I. Title.
BD311.K44 2007   204'.4   C2007-902672-9

Published by
NAMASTE PUBLISHING
P.O. Box 62084
Vancouver, BC, Canada V6J 4A3
www.namastepublishing.com
namaste@telus.net

Distributed in North America by
HAMPTON ROADS PUBLISHING COMPANY
Charlottesville, VA
hrpc@hrpub.com

Cover design: Amy King
Interior book design: Val Speidel
Illustrations: www.gabreyhl.com

Printed on recycled paper by
FRIESENS CORPORATION

Printed in Canada

To my beloved husband Howard,

My daughters Mary and Sarah,

My grandson Ethan, and

The late Sri Bijoux

CONTENTS

ACKNOWLEDGMENTS

I must firstly acknowledge Namaste Publishing's wonderful authors who have shared their presence and wisdom with me and the world. Anyone reading this book and familiar with Namaste Publishing's authors will see the undeniable contribution they have made to my growth in consciousness and therefore to this book.

So at one do I feel with Namaste Publishing's authors, so in sync with the truth they share, that I can hardly tell where I begin and they end. But this is one of the messages of *The Leap*. We cannot take singular credit for anything, as we are all one.

Next, I must extend deepest gratitude to David Ord, not only my latest author but my editor as well. It is wonderful to have had the tables turned and experience the importance of such a gifted and skilled editor. David's commitment to this book, his pressing work on it, always done with alacrity, has made the editing process a thing of joy. He has enriched this book and Namaste Publishing in so very many ways.

I want to thank Robert Friedman, President of Hampton Roads Publishing, for giving me access to the North American market for distribution of this book. I feel at one with him in our vision and purpose for publishing books in this genre. Here is a living example of what joining in noble intent can do.

Most importantly, I want to thank my beloved husband Howard whose faith in me and ongoing support have provided an unshakeable foundation upon which I have been able to take the leaps required to face life's challenges and opportunities with courage—however wobbly this courage has been at times.

NOTE TO THE READER

WRITTEN PURPOSELY in a concise manner, *The Leap* was not intended to be a quick read by the mind, but something that also speaks to the heart and spirit. Therefore, when reading *The Leap*, it is suggested that you take time to pause after each chapter—or even after each sub-section within a chapter—and integrate the content, not only at the mental comprehension level but also at the energetic heart level. These pauses could be for a few minutes, an hour, or even several days—the frequency and length of each pause to be determined intuitively by you.

PART I

THE LEAP

CHAPTER ONE

There Is Only One Way Out

HUMANKIND IS CURRENTLY trapped in a tragedy of its own making. We are stuck in repetitive cycles of conditioned human insanity such as warfare between nations, genocide, and wholesale slaughter among ethnic groups. There seems to be no end to the scourges of tribalism, child abuse, pornography, the suppression of women, and exploitation of the powerless—and, especially in our time, the destruction of Mother Earth herself. As the trampling of human rights and debasing of human dignity continue unabated in many parts of the world, we also continue to witness brutality on the streets of our cities, and violence even in our schools and our homes.

While the world spends trillions on weapons, millions continue to die of hunger, live in squalor, and suffer the ravages of disease.

It's not as if we didn't know any better—didn't know that aggression breeds aggression, killing more killing, neglect more severe problems. Neither is it as if there weren't plenty for everyone on this lush planet.

How can we not squirm in distress, even horror, when watching the evening news? Surely any thinking person can only blink with bewilderment as they ask themselves, "Can this be real? How is it that such barbarism can still be going on in our modern age?"

Far from feeling humiliation at what is happening, many of our species are in denial of the reality of our current human condition or express concern only when something negative impacts them directly. Some actually boast of their bigotry, racial prejudice, and sexism. They gloat over their ability to get away with fraud or to pull off hostile corporate takeovers where the "victor" requires subservience from the "defeated."

Everywhere we turn, the world is plagued by instability, and many live in perpetual fear. It is increasingly apparent that without a leap to a higher level of functioning, our species will be threatened with extinction in the near future.

Our past and present ways of responding to cries and crises—our own and those of humanity as a whole—are simply insufficient to halt what is increasingly feeling like a mad race toward self-annihilation. Many question whether there is in fact a way out of our madness.

Having said this, you may be surprised to hear that, in our era, I believe we will break out of this insanity and rise above our inhumanity—if we can demonstrate a radical level of global-wide caring never before seen on our planet.

How can I have such hope? What grounds are there for believing that, as a world, we will break free of our ages-long madness?

At the same time as we are seeing an escalation in the insanity of our species, we are also witnessing an increase in the opposite polarity. We are experiencing a flowering in the arts that makes the period of the

Renaissance pale in comparison. We are also seeing seemingly miraculous advances in the fields of science and medicine, together with an accelerating movement toward a more egalitarian distribution of the world's resources. Individuals of great wealth are contributing generously to noble causes. Pressure is mounting on every continent for the protection of human rights and the ending of dictatorships that oppress people. There is a growing movement toward environmental responsibility. Volunteerism is on the rise, with more and more people from affluent countries offering their services both in their own countries and abroad. These include medical and other professionals who at their own expense take time from their busy schedules to serve in Third World countries. We are also increasingly seeing the exposure and intolerance of corruption in all sectors—governmental, corporate, and religious. Coupled with these movements, we are witnessing more and more sincere efforts on the part of both those in leadership positions and the masses toward world peace.

Even more importantly, for the first time in our history, a new spiritual consciousness is rapidly emerging that is broad-based, planet-wide, non-sectarian, and inclusive of all. This higher level of consciousness is based on the realization that humans are essentially spiritual beings whose true nature is rooted in love.

This increase in consciousness is evident in my work as a publisher. I review many manuscripts that address issues related to consciousness. In the last two years, I have noticed a dramatic shift in the level of awareness from which these have been written. One of our authors, Eckhart Tolle, said that he has more hope for humanity now, after writing his third book *A New Earth* in 2005, than he did when he wrote his first book *The Power of Now* in 1997.

Everywhere, I see more people waking up to the need to do what they can to take positive, loving action in their lives. They realize that something must be done to break free of humankind's conditioned insanity in order to turn our world around. While taking what action they can within their own current spheres of influence, increasingly they are thinking globally.

At the close of World War II, General Douglas MacArthur, addressing the United States President and Congress, summed up the challenge before us: "Military alliances, balances of power, leagues of nations, all in turn failed, leaving the only path to be by way of the crucible of war. The utter destructiveness of war now blocks out this alternative. We have had our last chance. If we will not devise some greater and more equitable system, our Armageddon will be at our door. The problem basically is theological and involves a spiritual recrudescence, an improvement of human character that will synchronize with our almost matchless advances in science, art, literature, and all material and cultural developments of the past two thousand years. *It must be of the spirit if we are to save the flesh.*"[1]

I agree that our salvation as a planet will be found in the realm of spirit. But traditional spirituality will not suffice. Though the parliaments of the world pray for peace, and people on every continent march for peace, the reality of peace eludes us. Even when we intensify the earnestness and frequency of our prayers, meditations, and marches, we experience a frustration in not getting the results we need *now* to stop further pain, loss of lives, and destruction.

Could it be that there is something we are missing?

∼ The Leap

*I*T HAS BECOME APPARENT that the rapid healing of divisions that our world urgently needs will not come from stepping up our existing practices. Our species needs to take an evolutionary leap.

If you are reading this now, I believe that, intuitively, you know *we are the transition generation*—the ones to go beyond humanity's current repetitive insane acts and bridge to a more humane world. We don't have the time to wait for a subsequent generation to turn things around. As the Hopi Elders have so clearly reminded us: "We are the ones we have been waiting for."

This book invites you to take an evolutionary leap. By "leap," I mean a jump to a whole new level of functioning. Most of us have experienced taking a leap at some time in our lives. It might have been moving to a different community, launching into an entirely new career, moving on from a toxic work environment with no immediate job to go to, or leaving an unhappy marriage with no secure arms to fall into.

But what could this evolutionary leap *be*? I suggest that "be" is the germane word. As a species, we are being asked to take a leap in *consciousness*—to leave an unhealthy state of mind and ineffective practices that keep us stuck in our conditioned state, and to at last *be* what we are capable of *be*-ing as a species.

Let me illustrate the kind of leap that is entailed. *The Thin Red Line* is a movie about the realities of combat in the South Pacific during the Second World War. In one scene, a soldier is surveying a field after the battle of Guadalcanal. He is stunned by the grim carnage. Many of his comrades—some dead, some with gaping wounds, still others writhing in their limbless bodies in excruciating pain—are strewn on the ground like fodder for vultures.

Some pitch in to help the survivors, others stand or sit, stunned by the horror of what has just happened, their faces showing the shock at such insanity. As the narrating and witnessing soldier looks at his surviving comrades, he says, "Maybe we only have one big soul that everyone is a part of. Each face the same, man—like one big Self. Each one looking for salvation on their own, like coals thrown from the fire."

The soldier's words pierce to the heart of our human tragedy.

Our ability to solve our world's problems and our refusal to do so is due to our failure to see that we are all part of "one big Self." Instead, we are trapped in a belief that we are each separate individuals, pieces of coal thrown from the fire.

For the first time in human history, science is showing us a creation that is seamless. Space-time is a single fabric, encompassing all that exists. At the quantum level, there are no solid boundaries between any of the forms that make up our world. People, objects, mountains, rivers, galaxies, and even thought forms and feelings are all intimately interconnected. Like clouds of energy, we all rub up against each other, meld into each other, affect each other. All affects all, whether we consciously realize it or not. A change in a cell in your stomach can cause all the cells in your lungs to be affected. Pollution in one country can affect weather conditions in another. When a person coughs in Germany, it may not be long before someone catches a cold in Canada. Indeed, discovery of the principle of non-local cause reveals that we don't even need to be near each other to be affected by each other. When a person dies of starvation, on some level all experience the pain and sadness. Equally, when one person becomes more conscious, the whole of humanity becomes more conscious.

Simultaneous with the discovery that we are all part of a quantum soup, we have entered an era of almost universal access to print and electronic media, which is connecting us planet-wide in a network of oneness. Through science and technology, our growing awareness of our connectedness is opening the door to a global connectedness, giving us a glimpse of the kind of leap in consciousness that can transform our species and our world.

Our failure to see our connectedness, our oneness, causes us to behave as though we were each worlds unto ourselves, needing to struggle and defend ourselves against others in order to survive. This is the cause of all conflict and suffering, of all unease and disease of mind and body.

Because we have each participated in this unconscious state, we are each in some measure responsible for the mayhem of our world. We cannot simply blame others. Inasmuch as we have seen ourselves as separate, we have contributed our share to the insanity. If we do not see and accept that in some way we are part of the insanity, we can never hope to heal it.

An Impossible Dream?

A TRUTH THAT HAS BEEN APPARENT to some on our planet for a very long time is now being disseminated globally—and in the nick of time. This truth is spiritual in nature, and it has to do with our identity. When we truly understand our identity, we realize that even as we have each caused the condition our world is in, we are also each its savior. Because of this, we do not have to wait for others to bring about transformation. As we begin to live from our true identity, we *become* the transformation for which our world is waiting.

Viewing the world in its present fractured condition, a world united in oneness may seem an impossible dream—a utopian fantasy. But the Leap isn't a leap into fantasy. *It is a leap out of delusion and into reality.*

The oneness into which we as a species need to leap isn't something we have to create. It is already here in everyone on the planet. It is something we only have to awaken to and live.

There is an abundance of evidence that the Leap is a potential within all of us—an evolutionary development that can and must be realized now on a global scale.

Do you recall the sense of oneness that emerged all around the world on the day the Twin Towers in New York City collapsed? On every continent, millions came together in common grief, sensing that what was happening to the people of New York was in some way also happening to them. The 9/11 attacks spawned an ocean of compassion and goodwill toward the United States.

Though we act as if we were isolated individuals, and group together in our defensive enclaves with an "us" and "them" mentality, these are surface states that belie our most authentic humanity. Beneath the illusion of separateness, we long to experience the connection to each other that is far more fundamental to our nature than are our divisions. However, we can only connect in oneness with others when we have first connected with our true Self. This true Self of which I speak is the same true Self of others. It is the real heart and core of each and all of us. I call it our divine Self.

A few days after the 9/11 attacks on the World Trade Center, a colleague of mine was on his regular train commute home from New York City. The commuters were deep into their own worlds—reading newspapers, emailing from their Blackberries, staring out of the windows, nodding off. Suddenly, there were loud bomb-like sounds, as the sky turned an ominous dark grey. Coming on the heels of the attack on the Twin Towers, the explosive sounds startled everyone. The passengers, believing themselves to be targets of terrorists, were instantly abuzz with consternation. Complete strangers, shaken out of their isolation, were reaching out to whoever was nearby, questioning what was happening or reassuring each other. Just then the heavens opened up, signaling that the booms and darkening sky were caused by an imminent thunderstorm. As precipitously as the chatter had arisen, it ceased, and the commuters retreated once again into their isolated worlds.

My colleague commented how sad he felt that people when frightened, spontaneously reached out to one another yet withdrew their presence just as quickly once they realized their fear was unfounded. He began pondering what it would take for people to come together *without* the catalyst of fear.

In fact, what prevents the evidence of our inherent oneness from emerging all over the planet?

A Leap into Global Oneness

I THINK OF HUMANITY'S individualistic way of approaching life as *ego*. The ego is a picture of ourselves that we carry around in our head. It isn't who we really are at all; it's just a way of thinking of ourselves. And this way of thinking of ourselves, imagining ourselves to be vulnerable individuals, causes us to be oblivious of the fact that we are all one.

When we identify with ego as if it were who we really are, we simply can't see our oneness with the rest of our species, let alone our oneness with the whole created order. We don't recognize that we all have the same source that permeates the entire cosmos. This universal source is what I have in mind when I think of the divine. It's the oneness that science is unveiling, and that we are, through our communication technologies, catching a glimpse of on a worldwide scale. Even though the increased contact we have with each other up to this point is mostly at a surface level and lacks deep connection, the stage has been set.

The stranglehold of the ego is released when we enter into correct self-perception. I see this beginning to happen everywhere. Humankind is experiencing the throes of a massive shift in consciousness—the collapse of the false egoic mindset that has enslaved us, and an awakening to our divine Self.

The reaching out that emerged spontaneously on the commuter train leaving New York that day is beginning to happen not only between small groups of individuals, but also between nations. This is happening somewhat tentatively and sporadically right now, but let us hold to the vision that this coming together is destined to become a global reality. I feel that we are even now witnessing the emergence of situations—military, economic, and environmental—that will force us to begin relating to each other from oneness—albeit likely out of fear and necessity initially.

The urgency of shifting from a collective egoic mentality of "us" to one of "we" is evident when we look at some of humanity's current challenges, such as global warming, the threat of large-scale epidemics, terrorism, and nuclear proliferation. These reach beyond any sectarian or national boundaries, prompting the need for cooperation between world leaders. The world stage has been set for humankind to take the leap from thinking first nationally to thinking first globally. Our interdependence can no longer be denied. Other-interest *is* self-interest—global interest is national interest.

As our divine oneness, which is the true Self of all humanity, breaks through our imaginary disconnectedness, prizing open the vise-like grip of our egoic identity, we leave behind the sense of ourselves as separate little entities and leap to a consciousness of our connectedness. We leap from separation consciousness to unity consciousness.

As more and more of us see ourselves as one, the sense of connectedness that emerges will become a countervailing force that frees us from our insanity and the inhumanity that this insanity perpetrates.

Life speaks to us frequently of our oneness, but do we have eyes to see this evidence or ears to hear it? Once you become mindful of something in your life, by paying attention to it, you begin to see evidence of it everywhere. You are amazed you never noticed it before. This is because awareness in itself tends to draw to you repeated evidence of what you have now become aware of. So pay attention to the evidence of oneness in your life and note the increasing number of incidents that attest to this.

CHAPTER TWO

Stillness—The Foundation for the Leap

F ACED WITH THE SEVERITY of the world's problems, it is easy to succumb to feelings of helplessness and hopelessness. What can an individual do, we wonder, about disputes between nations, starvation in Africa, or tsunamis in the Indian Ocean?

We feel powerless in the face of the overwhelming power of an entrenched world order that is unconscious of our oneness as a species, a planet, a universe. We feel even more powerless when confronted with forces of nature that seem indifferent to human suffering.

As long as we are convinced that the world's problems lie outside of ourselves, we are unlikely to believe we can make a significant difference. If what is "out there" is quite separate from us, we will tend to see situations as largely immune to our influence. The best we can hope for then is to fiddle with effects, temporarily ameliorating the human condition but never really transforming it. Hence the widespread belief that "you can't change human nature."

Our sense of powerlessness is compounded by media hype, advertising, political propaganda, formalized religion, and even the very social activism that is intended to bring change. All of these are forms of self-delusion, in that they keep us focused on problems as if their causes were "out there" somewhere.

The leap our species needs to take involves a reorienting of our perspective. It involves realizing that all meaningful, all true change comes about first through *inner* work.

In trying to treat the problems we are facing, we ignore the only thing that actually matters—the quality of our inner state of *being*. It's here that the *cause* of our dysfunction lies. Consequently, solutions are always found on the inner plane. They emerge when we enter a place of heightened consciousness experienced in inner stillness, which is often called Presence.

The Power of Presence

WHAT CAN WE DO TO move to a higher state of consciousness?

It has been said that, one morning in Calcutta, India, Mother Teresa and her Sisters of Charity were running late for their visit to the first clinic on their daily round. As the cadre of nuns hurried along the streets of Calcutta that morning, Mother suddenly stopped in her tracks. Turning to her left, she looked down at a curb piled with streetside garbage. Walking over to the curb, she bent down. Out of the trash, she picked up a discarded premature infant, so small she could cradle it in the palm of one of her hands. The infant was in the crunched-up fetal position. As Mother Theresa gazed with love at this wee and weak creature, the child moved one arm then the other, one foot then the other, gradually opening fully like a flower to the warmth of Mother's love.

This story is sometimes recounted to show the power of the inclusive, unconditional love Mother Teresa extended wherever she went. I suggest that there is another important lesson to be gleaned from this incident.

The practice of the Sisters of Charity is to spend two hours at the beginning of each day in prayer and stillness. On this particular morning, they had spent more than the allotted time, which is why they were running late. Had Mother Teresa not spent so much time in stillness, would she have had the Presence to be alerted to the tiny manifestation of Presence by the side of the road?

When you live from Presence, you live from a higher state of consciousness. Because of this, you are connected to and can feel the Presence in everyone and everything. You come to see the other as *yourself*, and it is in this realization that our salvation lies. Eckhart Tolle said it beautifully: "The true meaning of love is to see the other as yourself."

When people join in a state of Presence, there is oneness. This is what the word "Namaste" in its extended definition means: "I honor the place in you in which the entire universe dwells. I honor the place in you which is of love, of truth, of light, and of peace. When you are in that place in you, and I am in that place in me, *we are one*."

∿ The Experience of Stillness

THE LEAP IN CONSCIOUSNESS we are about to take requires that we springboard into it from the foundation of inner stillness. This is what gives us the certainty that we are coming from our divine Self and bringing Presence into all that we do.

It is what affords us the assurance that what we need to know at any given moment will be given and that in our "doings" we will be guided and supported by the divine indwelling us.

Stillness is not silence. It is an intense awareness of our inner Presence. However, silence can be helpful in assisting us to more easily and quickly access our inner stillness, especially in the early stages of practicing entering into stillness. In Part II of this book, you will find practices to help you enter stillness.

As you cultivate inner stillness, you may notice that you naturally crave silence, the equivalent of stillness on the outer plane. This means that some of your habits are likely to change. You may find yourself drawn to quiet places instead of noisy environments. You may also find yourself declining invitations to noisy social gatherings with shallow conversation that is nothing more than mind chatter—mental noise. You may not listen to the car radio as much, and your interest in watching television may decline. You will likely become comfortable with more and more non-verbal yet deep communication in your relationships, as you start relating to others from a deeper place than surface thoughts and emotions. You will also experience an increasing delight in just sitting with yourself in stillness. Indeed, you will find that in stillness you are least alone.

How do you still the mind? By placing your attention on the present moment. A state of calmness arises in you when you do this. If you notice that you have drifted away from the present moment, bring your attention gently back to it. A quiet mind is unfamiliar to most of us, so we have to learn how to experience such a state. We will only recognize stillness after our mental chatter subsides.

It is important not to "effort" in order to bring your attention into the present moment. A still mind is not a forced mind. It is a mind at ease. Any effort to stay in the now comes from thinking about what you need to do, and thinking is not stillness. It is important not to make any judgment about how effective you are in holding to the present moment, because all such judgment involves thinking. You cannot break free from mental chatter by using your mind.

When you begin the practice of sitting in stillness, simply pay attention to the present moment. This is the opposite of concentration. Concentration is an exercise of thought. It requires a tight mental focus. By its nature it isolates and restricts. You cannot enter stillness by concentrating. Paying attention to the present moment is more of a full-body experience. There is a spaciousness about it. All you need do is observe. Notice what the present moment contains. Feel what it feels like. Witness your breathing. Be open to all of your senses.

To sit in stillness is to allow everything to be as it is. Exclude nothing from your awareness. This includes the whirring of the fan, the ticking of the clock, the noise of the traffic outside. It also includes any thoughts that come to you or emotions that arise. If you try to exclude anything from stillness, you are in resistance. It's impossible to be still and to be in resistance at the same time. So while you are abiding inwardly in stillness, you are aware of and accept everything that is taking place on the inner plane as well as in the outer world around you. Your intent is to become so anchored in stillness that you approach everything you do from this state of stillness. It is in stillness that the greatest power is released. That which cannot be grasped is at motionless work filling you with divine manna, which will nourish all of your conscious thoughts, words, and actions.

When you are inwardly still, you get in touch with your own essence. How good it feels to be who you truly are! Once you are in touch with the life within, you come to realize this same life force is within everybody. We all share in the same animating Presence. As you continue to spend time in stillness, cultivating awareness of your inner

Presence, you begin to *feel* that same Presence, that aliveness in the people and world around you, as did Mother Teresa.

An important meeting is before you, a key decision needs to be made soon, you feel wobbly after a crisis hits, or a situation has arisen unexpectedly and you don't know how to respond. Part II shows how to address such challenges by entering into stillness.

This purposeful entering into stillness is demonstrated by Jesus. The townsfolk caught a woman in the act of adultery and brought her to him to ask if they were not right in stoning her to death for breaking the law. The woman's accusers were certain they had Jesus cornered. Was he going to openly advocate breaking the law?

Jesus was on the spot. In that critical moment, how did he respond? Instead of panicking, he entered into stillness. Bending down, he began writing in the dust. We have no evidence of what he wrote, or even that he wrote anything meaningful. I see his writing in the sand as a delay tactic. The townsfolk wanted Jesus' response immediately, yet Jesus knew that he had to first go into stillness to access his answer. What came forth from that moment of stillness are some of the most powerful words ever spoken: "Let he who is without sin cast the first stone."[2] Presented with this challenge, the townsfolk themselves were now on the spot. One by one they slunk away, leaving the woman standing alone with Jesus.

All creation originates in stillness. Stillness is the field of infinite potentiality out of which we create our reality, our world. All fresh answers come out of stillness. It is through stillness that all perplexing issues are solvable. When we live our lives from the inside out, what I call our "inner knower" alerts us to all that we need to know. We stop seeking fulfillment outside ourselves, and we enjoy an inner contentment and confidence in living. The external fear-evoking world loses its hold on us.

How wonderful to abide in stillness, this no-thing that is the womb of everything. When we live from inner stillness, we are anchored in our divine Self. Then, anything we do in the world is imbued with divinity. The more we enter into stillness, the more our Presence perfumes all we say and do.

Accessing a Deep Wisdom

WHEN YOU ABIDE REGULARLY in stillness, you come to realize that there is no need to seek anything, including solutions, outside of yourself. It is in stillness that you access the omniscience of your inner knower. Just ask the question and watch for the answer or guidance to be given when it is needed, though perhaps not a moment before. You will *know* at the time you *need* to know.

I experienced this when, for over ten years, I was practicing as a management consultant. I was blessed with always working with colleagues who were spiritually conscious. Often before we entered a client's office, a boardroom, or a retreat center to facilitate a conflict resolution session, we allowed ourselves time to enter into stillness. During the facilitation that followed, we maintained this stillness. This enabled us to perceive the hidden oneness of everyone present at the meeting, which became the basis for identifying common interests and bringing people together.

Sometimes at these sessions we did little talking. We simply listened from a state of stillness, intervening only as stillness prompted. I expressed to my colleague after one such session, "It's hard to charge the client my full per diem rate, because on the outward activity level, I did or said almost nothing."

Frequently, when long-standing conflicts and ingrained office politics looked like they would win the day, my colleague and I would turn up the intensity dial on our inner stillness. Many times the situation appeared hopeless, yet the right guidance came to us from inner stillness, and what appeared to be miracles happened. Old hurts and entrenched negative patterns dissolved before our eyes, as conflicts were resolved and agreements reached—and almost always just in time for lunch!

I muse that, in the near future, stillness will be recognized as the way to solve differences and tackle our planet's problems. I envision a day when corporations, institutions, and governments, seeing the value of stillness, happily sanction "stillness breaks." Imagine a workplace in which people are truly present!

Presence is contagious. If you have only one or two people in a group who hold to Presence, it will affect the whole group. This is the power of an authentic spiritual teacher. Coming from a deep well of Presence, they invite others to join them there.

The power of Presence in just one individual can be seen in Herman Hess' *Journey to the East.* It is the story of various individuals who join together in a temporary community to go on a pilgrimage. Initially everything goes smoothly. The pilgrims get along together and cover a good distance every day.

The reader is soon introduced to a simple, quiet, happy, and unaffected fellow named Leo who always seems to be around at the right time, cheerfully helping out in whatever manner he can. There is something so pleasing and welcoming about Leo that everyone loves his presence.

Then one day Leo suddenly disappears without explanation. "Where did Leo go?" is the burning question. "And how could he leave without telling us?" A search party is formed to try to find him, but to no avail.

With Leo gone, relationships become strained. Bickering and arguing break out, becoming worse and worse.

The narrator, whom the reader assumes is Hess himself, soon loses interest in the pilgrimage and his quest. He abandons the group but carries with him an obsession with knowing more about Leo and the reason for his sudden departure.

This takes him on his own journey, a solo pilgrimage during which, no matter where he visits, he is always on the lookout for Leo and never abandons the hope that they will someday meet again.

Ten years pass before he stumbles across a lead—the name Andreas Leo, given to him by a person who is helping him with research on a project. The narrator sets out to discover whether this could indeed be the Leo he has been searching for all long. When he locates Andreas Leo, he stops him on the street, and they engage in conversation. Yes, this is the Leo who left the pilgrim group so many years earlier—but he does not recognize the narrator. Leo has to get back to his work, and the two part. Only later does the narrator find out that the unassuming Leo is actually President of the League that sponsored the pilgrimage in the first place.

The reader, like the actual pilgrims, becomes aware that Leo has something special within him that has such a positive influence on others—an ability to bring very different people together for a common goal. Robert Greenleaf, in *Servant Leadership*, attributes Leo's positive influence on others to the fact that he played a servant role within the group. The evolution of our consciousness now tells us that the "something very special" in Leo was his inner Presence. Exuding a strong field of Presence, he drew this same Presence out in other people.

On several occasions, I have shared this story when giving talks, encouraging participants to leave the workshop as Leos, bringing their healing Presence into their world.

∽ Stillness in the Corridors of Power?

ON A CHARTERED BUS TRIP through Ireland, three women engaged in conversation in response to a news article they had read that morning about global violence. "I do not see why such violence has to continue," said one of the women. "I do not see why we cannot live in peace."

The other two women reacted: "Oh, come on. You are talking Pollyanna. We are never going to change the way the world is. It's always been like this."

But the world has changed and can change. If you are reading this now, you surely must believe that there is a way to achieve world peace.

The potential for a shift from blame to taking responsibility for changing a situation can be seen in the case of Ireland itself, where peace has seemed elusive.

British Prime Minister Tony Blair's mixed legacy on the international scene is balanced by his negotiation of what became known as the Northern Ireland Good Friday Agreement. Though the situation appeared hopeless, Blair's sustained efforts and persistent personal intervention demonstrate how conflict that has raged for generations can be brought to an end when peace is our authentic intention. By incrementally implementing measures that all parties could agree to, Blair was able to introduce the people of this war-torn region to a modicum of peace. As Northern Ireland learned to enjoy the more relaxed atmosphere, further changes became possible. Finally, people came to realize how good it felt to live free of sectarian violence. They decided that violence can never again be a way of settling disputes—there is no longer a tolerance for it. Whatever the precise form Northern Ireland's government takes in the future, the people and the government are determined that it will be established through peaceful negotiations in a spirit of cooperation.

The last half century has taught us that even the most resistant of global crises are not beyond hope. In his book *Presidential Courage*,[3] Michael Beschloss, a leading presidential historian, relates how, during the Reagan era, tension between the United States and the Soviet Union had been escalating, much of it as a result of Ronald Reagan's rhetoric.

When the President was shot, there were fears it was a Soviet plot and the start of a nuclear attack. But rather than signaling aggression, the assassination attempt became a turning point in U.S.-Soviet relations.

Reagan began to believe that God had spared him for a purpose. First Lady Nancy told her husband that the confrontation between the two powers had become "ridiculous." She introduced him to Suzanne Massey, author of a history book about czarist Russia, who persuaded him that while the Soviets were dangerous, they were also human beings to whom he could relate.

Nancy Reagan and Suzanne Massey (who reminded Reagan of his mother) helped change the course of history. Influenced by these women, Reagan met with Andrei Gromyko. During the meeting, Gromyko suggested to Nancy that she whisper the word "peace" into her husband's ear every night. Agreeing to do so, she told Gromyko that she was whispering it into his ear also right there and then!

When meetings with Mikhail Gorbachev got underway, Reagan was severely criticized by many of his long-term supporters. They thought he had become a sentimental idiot. The President had to tell these critics, "Now don't worry that I've lost my bearings."

Reagan's willingness to listen to these two women led, in part, to one of the greatest shifts in global politics ever—the end of the Cold War and the tearing down of the Berlin Wall.

There are serious tensions in the world of the 21st century. The United States is in a standoff with North Korea. The situation had been growing increasingly tense, as North Korea tested missiles that could potentially deliver nuclear warheads. Then in 2007 a window opened for dialogue. Brokered by the Chinese and other concerned parties, nations spoke to each other directly around the negotiating table and glimpsed the possibility of solving their differences in a manner other than armed conflict. It remains to be seen whether this tentative first exchange between the hostile parties will bear fruit; much will depend on the goodwill of the key players.

In the wake of just a little progress with North Korea, the standoff over Iran's development of nuclear power seemed more hopeful. The United States had refused to speak directly to Iran. Now, the various parties could at least entertain that their refusal to dialogue was ultimately in no one's best interests, even though fear continues to dominate in their dealings. On another front, highlighting the possibility of a break with all precedent, a headline in the Toronto *Globe and Mail* announced, "U.S. open to separate dialogue with Arabs."

On a quite different front, but of equal if not greater relevance to our survival, Arnold Schwarzenegger, Governor of the State of California, has initiated the most far-reaching action to address global warming of any state in the Union. The Governor, showing enlightened leadership, kicked off an initiative that is not only inspiring other states but has also spread to Canada. His conversion to the need to arrest global warming is an encouraging sign, especially as other leaders pick up the torch.

Although these fledgling moves toward cooperation are a far cry from leaders sitting in stillness, they are harbingers of the new day that must dawn if we are to thrive as a planet.

When people come together and sit in stillness, surface differences can dissolve. As they go beyond the artificial barriers that separate them, they may become aware that they are each an expression of the same universal Presence.

When you are attuned to Presence, your oneness becomes evident. A peace can then enter the relationship. You are given the opportunity to let go of former experiences and judgments of each other, becoming open to new directions and fresh ways of relating.

Let's envision the day coming, and coming soon, when the world's leaders sit together in stillness prior to, and periodically during, their deliberations. When their course of action is unclear, there will be no haggling or jockeying for national advantage, no cajoling, haranguing, or threatening. They will know it is time for a different kind of ceasefire and enter into a tryst with stillness.

Whenever creative solutions are required so that the needs of all are met, leaders will retreat from the world to replenish their souls. By entering into stillness, they will be able to leave their habitual thinking patterns behind, creating space for new perceptions to guide them. Retreating into stillness is always followed by a creative phase. Out of this "time out," novel solutions to longstanding problems can arise. By entering into stillness and invoking a deep spiritual wisdom, the leaders of the future will *know* the noble course to take.

Jesus recognized the power of retreating into stillness. The night before his crucifixion, face to face with the most important decision of his earthly life, he went into the Garden of Gethsemane to pray. A stone's throw from his disciples, he uttered an agonizing request. It was addressed to his true Self—the Presence he called "My Father." Was there any way to avoid the execution that lay ahead of him? This was the only question he asked. Then, he became still and waited.

After an hour, he checked on his disciples, who had fallen asleep. Again going aside to be alone, he uttered the same words, becoming silent and waiting yet another full hour.

Again checking on the disciples, who were still sleeping, he returned to pray a third time, asking the same question. There was no proliferation of words and no begging or pleading, simply the one question.

As Jesus' thoughts quieted down and his emotions became still, the answer finally came. If he was to maintain his integrity, living in the world in the only way to be true to himself, he knew what he must do. Once this clarity—this certainty—came from his inner knower, he went forward to his crucifixion without regret and in complete surrender.

∽ *Our Need for a Noble Vision*

The Leap IS ADMITTEDLY a visionary book, but necessarily so, for "where there is no vision, the people perish."[4]
As a consultant, I was often hired by organizations that felt they were stuck in long-standing management, operational, and personnel issues, which prevented them from realizing their full potential. In many of those instances, I suggested that the organization first go through a larger visioning process before turning to the more specific issues of concern. Upon their agreement, we scheduled a time to dialogue and articulate the envisioned state of the organization. Next, we determined the specifics of their current state of reality. After that, everyone could see the gap—often huge—between their current reality and their vision for the organization. We then worked at identifying what would be needed to close the gap. At this point, the many specific steps required to achieve this became evident. So now we had an overview of a plan with which everyone was familiar and all agreed, enabling us to move forward.

The need to change was evident, and the readiness to change was there, given the degree of dissatisfaction with the current organizational state. What was now needed was the requisite commitment to close the gap. Level of commitment is something that cannot be measured at the start but can only be determined once you see the people take sustained action to attain the vision state.

It is up to each of us to create a vision for our personal world, then live our lives in such a way that we start closing the gap between what we are currently experiencing, which falls short, and our vision of what we would like to see. This is what the Leap is asking us to do—establish a vision of what our highest self wants, then take action to make it a reality.

When you are engaged in something, or are drawn into a situation or argument, ask yourself the question: "What does this have to do with the leap I want to make?" The causative level of everything is within. We can be so tempted to address external issues and believe that by fiddling with effects, we are making changes. But nothing really changes unless the change is initiated from our inner being.

Causes we become involved in need to flow from our inner state, concurrent with our deepening consciousness. There are many noble causes. However, if we are not attentive, we can let ourselves get drawn into all sorts of diversions. Making the Leap requires a focus, an ongoing attention to our vision. The Leap points us back to our inner work—shifts in perception, acceptance of truth—which only we can accomplish.

I muse that soon there will be a level of international leadership that will articulate a noble global vision for all of humanity, then call on each and every one of us to move—together—towards achieving that vision.

Do dream. Dream of the time when the leaders of nations function not from fear, but from inner Presence. Dream of a world in which we deal with each other from a sense of our oneness as a species. Dream of each and every one of us accepting the responsibility of being custodians of human life and of this planet.

Imagine what could emerge if, instead of posturing to save face before their publics, the emissaries of nations set aside issues of national and personal ego and sought solutions that would benefit all concerned. Imagine if, individually and collectively, they entered into stillness … and from *there* sought answers to the world's troubles.

As Henry David Thoreau told us, we should go right ahead and build our castle in the air—as long as we remember after doing so to put the foundation under it.

⌒ *Take Vision into Stillness*

*I*T ISN'T THE WEALTHY, the powerful, the famous who are going to solve our planet's problems. Not even education, helpful though it is, will bring us the global solutions that are needed today. Pursuing these paths has only served to highlight the inability of our minds and actions to move beyond our divisions. It is time for us to recognize that *stillness* is the way.

Stillness is causative. It is creative. All fresh and new ideas come out of the womb of inner stillness, since in stillness we are able to tap into universal consciousness. This is vastly more reliable than the solutions that come from the limited, conditioned, thinking mind that almost always bases its solutions on what was relevant in the past, not on what is most appropriate for the present situation.

When stillness is our foundation, we don't hungrily look outside of ourselves and grab for answers, but rather allow for insights and solutions to emerge naturally from within us. We allow our unconditioned inner knower to correct our perceptions and to guide our thoughts, dialogues, and efforts until positive solutions come.

CHAPTER THREE

"Inner Knower" as Our Source of Guidance

ONE OF THE BLOCKS we experience to receiving guidance from our inner knower is our tendency to seek answers outside ourselves. In our western world, idolatry of individuals who are considered leading lights in society is rampant, as attested to by our glorification of politicians, celebrities, movie stars, wealthy executives, sports and entertainment figures.

Anyone who is lionized by the masses knows they have no answers to give others. They can only share their own experiences, their own reality, their truth as they see it. Yet very few of them tell their supporters or fans to turn their attention away from them and back to themselves. However, this is what the true spiritual teacher always does. "Don't look at me, don't adulate me," says the true teacher. "See the magnificence in your own essence. Know that you already know what I am sharing with you."

When another shows you something about yourself, this is not the same as self-discovery. Unless your own consciousness grasps the truth of the insight, it doesn't have the power to transform you. Others may point the way or mirror something to you about yourself, but only to the degree that what someone shares triggers your own inner knowing does it liberate you from your conditioning. How sad then that we have become so influenced by the external world and rarely look inside ourselves for direction. Yet here alone do we meet the causative dimension of our experiences. Guidance must come from within. It cannot come from a teacher or guru.

Neither is guidance assured when it comes from use of a technique. Just as we fall into different metabolic types, so also we have different temperaments and therefore find some techniques helpful and others unproductive. Because we are all unique, a technique that is helpful to one may be a form of bondage to another. Only when a technique facilitates the awareness and expression of our authentic being is it helpful.

You might imagine that your beliefs are a safe guide. But think about how a person's beliefs may evolve during the course of a lifetime. Many of us find ourselves holding quite different beliefs in mid-life from those we held when we were young. One of the difficulties Jesus' peers experienced with him was his more enlightened approach to his nation's understanding of values. The Sermon on the Mount proposes some radically different ways of behaving than were customary for most people at the time. How did Jesus know that some of the practices he advocated were better than those many had followed for centuries? He was guided solely by "the Father within"—his inner knower.

Most of us are not yet in the habit of seeking guidance from our inner knower, preferring to stay with the more familiar approach of mental analysis or relying on what we think of as our "feelings." These are too often conditioned emotions rather than the true feelings emanating from the wisdom of the heart.

By their very nature, most thoughts distort perception and therefore what is real. Though appearing to originate in the moment, thought is generally conditioned by the past. This is because thought tends to be made up of memories. When we think, though we imagine we are thinking new thoughts, most of the time thought is nothing more than a rearrangement of the memories stored in our brain. We select memories and join them in an order we deem logical. Even though the mind strings memories together in an array of patterns, its range of reference is nevertheless limited. It cannot come up with anything truly original unless the thinking arises from inner awareness. In fact, the thinking mind often cannot even clearly perceive what is happening in the present because it sees through windows tainted by the past. This is why all innovation and true progress is born from the womb of Presence. We may believe it is the thinking mind that has come up with new ideas, but the mind is just the recipient of and channel through which these new insights are expressed.

How ironic that we seek to know through our own limited and conditioned thinking, when it is conditioned thinking that led us into confusion in the first place. To think about our thoughts and feelings prevents us seeing ourselves accurately as we are right now, which is an extension of our divine Source. No wonder self-awareness cannot come from mental analysis! When we go deep within ourselves, we discover another dimension—the realm of stillness. Awareness of our divine Self emerges from this state of inner stillness. This is the home of our inner knower, which contains no thoughts. Because it is free of thought, it is not conditioned by past experiences. It is from this source that true insight arises.

Our inner knower's role is to correct our perceptions, thereby bringing us back to experience the peace that is our natural state. When we feel peace, we know that we are seeing with accurate spiritual vision. Whenever we are not at peace, our perception is skewed.

Our inner knower shows us when we are projecting our own negativity onto another. At such a time, we will simply not feel at peace. This may manifest as anger, resentment, criticism, defensiveness, fear, and so on.

Our inner knower not only shows us when we are projecting onto another, but also when someone is mirroring back to us a quality of our true nature. For example, when we experience generosity in someone else, we are seeing the generosity within ourselves. When we witness compassion, gentleness, and goodness in another, we are witnessing a mirroring of our own level of compassion, gentleness, and goodness. We can only see these things according to the level we ourselves have developed.

Opposites don't attract. Like attracts like. I once asked a woman what she loved most about her husband. She responded, "His strength, his integrity, and his goodness." What she couldn't see was that she too embodied these qualities. It took a number of years for her to come to this realization. As she did, I noticed that her husband was also realizing that he embodied the things he most loved about his wife. When we fall in love with someone, we are seeing through the outer to the inner beauty of the person, which draws us because it is a reflection of who *we* are. In essence, then, we always only fall in love with our Self.

This principle of recognizing ourselves in others applies even when an angry, negative person is attracted to a spiritually conscious person. Beneath their negativity, there is an awareness of their own fundamentally peaceful and loving divine Self. If there weren't, they would not be attracted to the peace and love in another.

If you see a number of angry people in your life, how can you know whether you are projecting your anger onto them, or they are being attracted to your inner peace? You will know by whether, when you are around them, you become upset and reactive, or maintain your peace.

∼ *Learning to Trust My Inner Knower*

*H*OW CAN WE KNOW WHEN an answer is coming from our inner knower? When our inner knower responds to us, we will know it to be the authentic voice of spirit because it will evoke no fear in us. Instead, we will relax into the "knowing." There is no uncertainty in the knowing, no further questioning, no room for doubt or hesitation.

If we are guided by our inner knower to take action, it will be action likely done with grace and ease. It will lead to healing or some other positive outcome, not only for ourselves but for all concerned.

When we go within and pose a question or make a request for guidance, we must be prepared to be patient. Sometimes we ask and the answer comes almost instantly or shortly thereafter. Sometimes, as we shall see, we need to ask again, and perhaps again. At other times we need to wait, to listen, and to watch. Why watch? Because our inner knower often speaks to us not only through the still inner voice, but also through things that happen in our lives—people who come into our lives, what they say to us, incidents that occur, "signs" that may come to us from varied sources, including nature and repetitive occurrences.

Our inner knower is charged with correcting our perceptions, because we often misperceive through the eyes of the ego. When we do this, it will speak to us through a change in perception. This may not bring about a change in our outer situation, but it will bring about inner change, and this will result in a sense of peace. So don't hesitate to ask your inner knower to correct your perception whenever you are not experiencing peace. Many of us have already had the experience of having our perception corrected by our inner knower and can say with gratitude, "You know, nothing has really changed, but everything has changed."

When we receive guidance from our inner knower, we find ourselves relaxing into a situation, a relationship, or life in general. We feel more expansive, more confident, and clearer in our direction—and often we find the courage to act that we never thought we had.

The more we ask of our inner knower, the more readily we develop our inner ears to hear its voice, and the more confident we become in living our life from the inside out—as it was always meant to be lived. This security is needed especially in these times of confusion and high uncertainty. With the widespread availability of information through various forms of media and the worldwide web, never before have there been so many outside voices to listen to, and never before have they seemed to be more varied and conflicting.

Experiment with your inner knower. Start first by asking for help with simple things such as finding your glasses. Then ask it if there is anything in a serial dream you have been having over several months that would be helpful for you to "see." Ask for help in writing a paper for your English Literature class, then wait for the inspiration to flow.

When you bring a large life issue to your inner knower, such as whether you are to leave a marriage or change careers, you will likely have to pose your question again and again until the situation changes and the question is no longer relevant, or until you are "ready" to hear the guidance.

It is also likely that the guidance will be given in stages and not all at once. This is because our inner knower never reveals anything that may bring fearful reaction instead of peace. It always knows what we are ready to accept at any particular time.

⟨⟩ The Wand of Consciousness

IN JOSEPH MCMONEAGLE's autobiographical account *Memoirs of a Psychic Spy,* he relates how his inner knower kept him from death during his stint in the Vietnam War. In times of great danger, when every cell in our body is on full alert, and we are forced into present moment awareness, we may have heard the unquestionable guidance of our inner knower just as McMoneagle did. He writes:

What is material about my time in Vietnam is how much I came to rely on my gut or intuitive nature. Many times I instinctively knew I wasn't safe, or that I was somehow exposed to danger. The small voice inside my gut became a lot louder and I listened. Inside and outside the base camp, I always listened to my inner voice, did whatever it suggested, and did it without question. If I felt an urge to get into a bunker, I did so immediately. If it was a gut feeling to zig rather than zag, then that's what I did. I once abandoned a Jeep and walked back to the base camp on advice of my internal voices. To the consternation of my first sergeant, the Jeep was never seen again.

While sitting in a listening post one night near a small unit outside of Tay Ninh, I had a terrible urge to move. The small voice in my gut was telling me to be anywhere but there. Movement was difficult because it was pitch black—the kind of dark where you can't see your hand right up in front of your face. I had to convince the two others who were there it was the right thing to do. It took almost an hour, but we shifted west of our original position by about sixty yards. Around 4:00 A.M. we heard a series of grenades going off in the area we had previously occupied.

During a firefight at LZ Two Bits, just north of Qui Nhon, I took up a gun position on top of a bunker facing the village just outside the wire. Within minutes my inner voices were screaming at me, "Be somewhere else!" I shifted to a firing slot inside the bunker. Seconds later the top of the bunker was racked with two direct hits from mortar rounds. My voices started yelling again, "Not enough! Get out!" So I quickly moved through the bunker entry, sliding sideways to a depression in the ground. I just cleared the bunker doorway when an RPG (a high-explosive rocket-propelled grenade) opened the bunker up like a banana hit with a sledgehammer. My voices kept me moving all night long.[5]

What strikes me about this account is that McMoneagle did not question or second guess his inner knower—an indication that he had already built a trusting relationship with it. His experiences of the saving power of his inner knower encourage us not to wait until a time of extreme personal danger to start developing this innate sense, which until now has either remained latent or only working at partial capacity in most of us. Several gifts, such as clairvoyance, clairaudience, and clairsentience, await our experience once we have shed the self-imposed limitations of the egoic self and opened to the vastness of our divine consciousness.

There is nothing that you and I face in our private lives, or that we face as a world, to which consciousness does not have the answer. This is true even of situations pertaining to the natural world.

We attribute natural disasters to Earth itself, on the assumption that nature is its own master. Our belief that nature behaves unpredictably with sheer blind force is so deeply entrenched, it seems heresy even to question it. However, there is growing evidence that our oneness extends beyond the human species to all living things on the planet, and even to the so-called "inanimate" world, including our Mother Earth.

On December 26, 2004, the massive Asian Tsunami killed over a quarter of a million people in the coastal towns and villages of nine countries surrounding the Indian Ocean. Despite the huge human death toll, Sri Lanka's Yala National Park, home to elephants, leopards, and monkeys, reported no mass animal deaths in the wildlife reserve. Much of the wildlife fled to higher ground in the hours before the region was struck by the tidal wave. How did animals detect the tsunami ahead of its arrival?

Although subsequent research doesn't indicate a "sixth sense" in animals, as some have proposed, it does confirm that the creatures of the region were more *aware* of subtle environmental changes than were their human counterparts. Just how animals sense environmental changes ahead of humans is still uncertain. Vibratory changes on land and in water, running via the deep sound channel, would have given close to two hours warning in the case of the Asian Tsunami. Electromagnetic changes in the atmosphere would have provided about thirty minutes warning. Animals were responsive to these, it seems, whereas humans generally were not. This shows that there is a connection between the seemingly blind forces of nature and consciousness, though at this time most of us, with the exception of children, are insufficiently aware to notice. Children are closer to feeling their connection with all that is.

A woman from the Netherlands related this experience:

> Last year, I arrived at school to pick up the kids some ten minutes before the due time. It was a beautiful, bright sunny day, and as I crossed the gate I saw that my daughter's class was still at the playground enjoying such a rare day. I approached her teacher and commented on the fact that the children must have had a great morning because of the weather. The teacher answered that, to the contrary,

the kids were restless and difficult to cope with. She then added, to my surprise, that we were heading for a storm at the end of the day. She indicated that such type of behavior in children was a clear sign of weather changes. My reaction, based on forgetfulness of what we are, was that this was impossible, considering that the weather forecast did not foresee any such situation for the day. She laughed and said, "Just wait and see." Indeed, at the end of the day, we had one of the most violent wind storms ever. Thousands of trees fell on the ground, causing much damage and some deaths. Many walls that divided the motorways from living areas fell apart, creating lots of problems. The government advised us not to get out of our houses if we did not need to.

Children and animals have not yet restricted their access to their inner knower. We adults seem to have suppressed this innate ability. As our ego developed, we deemed other things more important.

CHAPTER FOUR

Your Finger Only Points at You

WHEN WE DON'T FEEL SAFE in the world, it's as if we were back in the Garden of Eden, imagining we could actually do something to offend God and thereby cut ourselves off from our divine Source. With this misperception comes fear, as evidenced in metaphoric terms in the story of Genesis when it states that as soon as Adam and Eve believed they had done something wrong against God, they covered themselves out of a sense of shame. How could we possibly do anything wrong against God, when we are one with God? We must have believed we could actually offend our Self, and this opened the door for self-judgment, which is the basis of all judgment.

There Is No Room for Judgment
in Higher Consciousness

FUNDAMENTALLY, ALL JUDGMENT stems from the erroneous belief that we are completely separate beings, needing to protect ourselves against other people, difficult situations, and painful experiences because we see ourselves as vulnerable to attack from outside forces. In essence, we have judged that to be alive at all is to be at risk of attack from "out there." In concluding this, what we have really done is judged life itself to be threatening and therefore something to be feared. And that is the kind of world we have created. When we do not believe in the benign, loving, supportive nature of life, we severely limit our ability to experience it as such.

Judging has become so interwoven with the fabric of our lives that we often are not aware we are doing it. There seems to be nothing that escapes our judgment—people, self, situations, and experiences. When we judge, we are saying we don't want something in our life because we *think* it doesn't match our desires or expectations. Since the ego is perpetually not happy with things as they are, always wanting and needing more or something else, we take some of its food away, so to speak, when we stop judging.

Not judging opens the door to appreciation. If you have only a crust of bread to eat, you can judge it as not being sufficient, or you can eat it with appreciation and thanksgiving, thereby transforming it into a feast. If you begrudge the fact that you have only three dollars in your pocket, why would your divine Self give you ten? Acceptance, appreciation, and thanksgiving open the floodgates for the abundance of your divine Self to flow into your life. Judging something also means you are resisting it, which shuts off your ability to receive divine blessings from it. This is why in the Christian tradition, thanksgiving, especially in situations that don't seem at all to call for it, is often considered the highest form of prayer.

We are never happy when we judge another because judgment separates us from our sisters and brothers, making us superior and the other inferior. When we judge others, we are actually saying that we are right and they are wrong. This is an activity of ego, not of our loving Self. It fosters separation through rejection. We can never be fully at peace when we have put another out of our heart. When we identify with our false egoic self, we believe that by attacking others, we are able to make ourselves stronger and less vulnerable to attack from them. This is an illusion.

Judgment isolates and distorts because it never sees the whole and thereby what is good about the person, thing, or situation being judged. This includes when we judge ourselves.

If we judge a situation because it disturbs or hurts us, we are again in the hands of ego. Since judgment is based on fear, not love, out of our fear we are likely to create the thing feared. When we come from fear, we come from resistance to what is. This separates us from the reality of what is and in so doing prevents us from bringing our healing Presence to the situation.

But what if I am suffering from a sore leg—am I to bless this situation and be thankful for it? In any painful or upsetting situation, the most self-loving response is acceptance of it because this keeps us from falling into egoic fear. If you then also bring authentic gratitude and blessing to this situation, regardless of how it appears, you keep the gates of divine grace open, allowing blessings to flow into the situation and you.

What about when tragedy strikes? This is the acid test of whether we really have come to awareness of our true nature. If we can see through tragedy to the underlying larger plan of the one divine Self—if we truly believe that everything is from love—then love, and only love, is what we will experience. We will find the succor, the good in tragedy, and build on it until we have eliminated all tragedy from the human condition. This is the treasure that is buried in pain and tragedy. This is the power of the Crucifixion. This is why it is usually at our lowest point that we are visited by grace.

C.S. Lewis, in *A Grief Observed*, describes how he was once again able to believe in a loving God when, after a long period of feeling inwardly dead through grieving the loss of his wife, he was suddenly surprised by joy. It flooded in without cause, without being bidden, and with no announcement. Nothing, including what seemed like a bottomless pit of grief, could negate the existence of his divine nature. It was always there, just awaiting the opportunity to once again be recognized.

Often we experience the influx of grace when we are in challenging conditions—when we hear that we need a serious operation, or someone close to us dies, or some other tragedy strikes. It is then that a gentle and buoying energy appears to envelop, support, and protect us. Challenged by the human condition of being vulnerable in our bodies, the reality of our spiritual Self breaks through to remind us that our body is not all we are but only a vehicle for experiencing our divine self in human form. Grace comes rushing in when the door of the ego—our sense of individualism—crashes down.

∽ Blame Be Gone

WHEN WE BLAME, WE RESIST someone or something in our life because we feel they are responsible for our irritation, pain, or unhappiness.

When you don't blame the weather for the fact that you are feeling low, you may come to see that you are really "using" the grey, rainy day to help you release unexpressed pain over some loss in your life—perhaps the recent loss of your job or a beloved pet. In this way, you can acknowledge and be thankful for the healing process the dull day facilitates.

When you don't blame your parents for your feeling separation anxiety, you may come to see the root of it is your sense of separation from divine Source. Then go on to realize you can never be separated from the divine Self that you are.

When you don't blame the dog for disturbing your sleep, you acknowledge your lack of sleep but don't mix it with anger and fuel it with resentment the following day, thereby increasing the drain on your energy.

Blaming puts up a wall that prevents us from seeing what we are creating in our lives and why. It is disempowering when we ascribe the control over our circumstances and feelings to someone or something else. When we feel justified in our blaming, we are just finding an excuse for not taking responsibility for our lives the way they are. It isn't possible to blame and feel divinely empowered at the same time.

Acceptance of what is, when on the surface it looks like we should not accept a situation, is an act of faith and self-love. It allows a transforming energy to enter the situation. If this does not alter the outer experience, it will certainly change our inner landscape. We will experience a softening and opening within ourselves that allows us to embrace the situation instead of railing against it.

Take the incident of a daughter sitting with her aged father who had physically and emotionally abused her as a child. Up until that time, she could not accept that anything good had come out of her relationship with her father. On this occasion, her father was relating a story of self-pity. The daughter, knowing she may never again have time to sit with him alone before he died, this time simply listened from inner stillness without resistance to him or judgment of any kind. She told me that soon she wasn't a daughter listening to her father, or even a female listening to a male, but a field of Presence blending with another field of Presence. In that moment, she felt nothing but love for and oneness with her father. This is spiritual communion. In this communion of oneness, we find peace. Her father died a few months later, leaving her with no regrets or pain from the past, just a memory of the love they both felt in their final oneness.

Let's hold to the vision that the triumph of oneness over judgment and blame experienced by this father and daughter will soon be experienced on a much wider scale.

∼ Scapegoating Is Self-attack

SCAPEGOATING IS AN INDIRECT means of self-attack, self-criticism, and even self-loathing. When we blame with vehemence—when we don't own in any measure the fault we see in others—this is a sure signal that we are using another as a scapegoat. Our own negative states are being reflected back to us in the other.

By using another as a scapegoat, we attempt to free ourselves of blame and responsibility. But we are never free of the effects of our own creations—it is only an illusion to think that we are. On the contrary, when we scapegoat, we are reacting fearfully to someone or some situation and thereby giving it power over us.

It is little wonder that we scapegoat so readily, when even Jesus' apostles indulged in scapegoating. When Jesus was taken by the Romans, Judas, the apostle who betrayed him for 30 pieces of silver, became a scapegoat—hence the term "Judas-goat" was coined. A Judas-goat serves as a reminder to us of how we use projection to purposely blind ourselves to our own character traits, and to absolve ourselves of responsibility for what we see in our world that we do not like and judge to be wrong.

Who among the rest of the apostles did not betray Jesus? When the Roman soldiers came to the Garden of Gethsemane to take him away to the Roman Governor Pontius Pilate for arraignment, most of the apostles fled and later denied Jesus by hiding their association with him. Yet Judas became the scapegoat for them all. Who among us has not in some way betrayed the gentle and loving beings in our lives at some time or another?

Wasn't Jesus himself also a scapegoat for the many who could not accept his light and the unquestionable truth he taught? Because they could not face up to the darkness in themselves, they had to project it outwards onto Jesus in order to accord themselves a false absolution.

Jesus shows us how to respond to those who use us as scapegoats. In spite of what was done to him, he never cast anyone out of his heart. During his passion, Jesus went right on loving and caring for those who had made him a scapegoat. He was able to do so because he remained anchored in awareness of his invulnerability as his divine Self. He was invulnerable because he knew he was not his body, so no ultimate harm could come to him. Of course Jesus resurrected! How could it be otherwise when *who he truly is* was never killed? Only his body was crucified. When we also have this awareness, we can respond lovingly to those who unjustly attack us.

We don't quite know how to respond to those who have no egoic self-concept to defend, who just stand in service to what life presents to them in the moment and choose to always come from love. But they *do* leave their lasting impact on us.

Pontius Pilate must have been deeply affected by his encounter with complete non-judgment from the man he turned over to mob-judgment. Similarly, the Roman soldiers who participated in Jesus' crucifixion surely must have left the cross as sadder but wiser men.

In modern times, we love to use politicians as scapegoats. If we truly owned our own creations and didn't like what we saw, we would instead pray for our politicians, intending that they become the kind of leaders who will bring into reality our most loving intentions for humanity and our Mother Earth. Then we would live our own lives doing the same.

The world of the 21st century is preoccupied with fear of terrorism. Terrorism reflects a scapegoat mentality, both on the part of the terrorists and on the part of the populace that fears terrorism. This means that, whenever we are under attack from terrorists, we are in some measure participating in their terrorism. Though this may be difficult for many to accept, an act of terrorism is not simply an act committed against us, it is an act that we and/or our ancestors in some way contributed to. Who among us can say that they do not have "attack thoughts" towards others? In the terrorist these feelings are simply magnified then acted on.

If you see the terrorist "out there," you must have some of the terrorist within you. This is true also of the criminal, the con artist, the greedy, and so forth. There is no exception. We like to think of such people as "them," as if they were sub-human, but they are also us. These outer "villains" serve to remind us that there are parts of us as individuals and as a species that are in need of healing. Unless we own these negative states, these shadow aspects of ourselves, how can we possibly bring healing love to them?

If you can look at the one who commits terrorist acts and see a person who is acting out of spiritual unconsciousness, and who is crying out for love, then you open *yourself* to spiritual healing as well. It is only when we do this as nations that we will be able to heal our world of its divisions.

Eliminating terrorism begins with altering our perception of the other. We must see the other as part of us, and reach out in a spirit of love. Terrorism, a group act, will not be eliminated, however, until we come together and recognize how, as societies, we *collectively* project onto a group of people characteristics that we do not want to face up to in ourselves.

We are responsible for how we respond to all we see and experience. We have drawn everything into our life, intending it as it is. When we come to see and accept this, we will then naturally turn our attention to weeding, watering, and caring for our inner garden. Through complete self-love, which will eliminate all negativity and lead to expressing our divine attributes, we will surely bring in a heavenly harvest on earth.

Being Versus Drama

WHEN WE DON'T KNOW WHO we truly are, we make up stories about ourselves in the hope of finding ourselves. In these dramas, we are the protagonist and all others are our supporting cast.

Stories about ourselves take the place of living a *real* life. When we are deadened to the inner life of Spirit, we create drama for ourselves in order to experience some semblance of life, even if it is a false sense of life. Our stories are a means of feeling that something "important" is happening. We have become a race of storytellers, not real livers of life.

What kind of story have you created about yourself? Are you the millionaire industrial magnet? God's gift to women? The perfect mother? The unemployed drug addict? The defrocked priest?

Because of our ego's need to feel secure, we identify with a fragmentary expression of the one Self, even if it is an unhappy self, as if it were the whole. We take this image of ourselves to be who we are. We then hang onto this false sense of self for dear life.

If you listen to your own stories, you will see that the predominant themes running through them are that of victor and victim. The self-indulgent ego relishes both roles—if it can't play one, it will happily play the other. We welcome the opportunity to tell others about our achievements and our pain, especially our pain.

Note what happens when you drop the role of either victor or victim. Where is the separation then? What if you looked at the disheveled beggar on the street and did not see a victim, someone to pity or feel guilty about? What if you did the same with the woman dying of cancer or the injured soldier? What would you see then? How would you act toward them then?

When we can't manufacture enough stories in our own life to keep up the facade of really living, we also live vicariously through the drama of others. We turn to soap operas, reality television shows, and gossip. Indeed, the media in North America is little other than a storybook of egoic dramas. How people love to get in front of the camera and tell their stories, particularly those sad stories that justify their victim roles. Poor me. Poor you. Or how I overcame poor me and now am victorious me.

Your story is made up of past events in chronological order. The egoic mind's habitual pattern is to go back and forth along this life-line of events and look for a place to reactivate something by bringing the past into the present. The victim and victor cannot exist without the past. Try dropping your sad story and you will drop your pain. Even your most recent story of who did what to you yesterday.

If you feel any dissonance, angst, resentment, worry—in short, if you are experiencing any psychological pain—try stepping out of your story. Just do it. Step out. Drop the past. Don't go to the event or series of events from which the "story of you" is derived. What will be left will be some residual uncomfortable feeling that will soon fade away. The pain or discomfort cannot survive without the story. If the mind comes in and tries to start the story once more, simply say, "Mind, be still."

You can spend your whole life stuck in the tangle of your stories, often repeating the same tales over and over again. Actually, when you look at the stories we tell ourselves, you will notice that there are not that many stories out there. I've made it, you haven't. I've been abandoned. I am unlucky. My lover left me. No one appreciates me. I have a fatal illness. Different casts, but the same stories.

Observe yourself. See what stories you tell yourself or tell others. Notice how you hang on to your drama even when it brings you pain. Indeed, one of the most immediate rewards of dropping drama from our lives is that we experience a whole new level of energy. Keeping the drama going is draining.

When we tell ourselves a story that causes us emotional or psychological pain, Byron Katie, author of *Loving What Is*, suggests we ask ourselves: Is this true? Are you sure it is true? If it brings you pain, is there one good reason to hang onto this story? What would happen if you dropped it?

"I have come that they may have life, and that they may have it more abundantly," said Jesus.[6] When you choose to drop drama, you will find real life is so much more fulfilling. Drop the need to take revenge on the thief who broke into your home, and you will find peace. Drop your worry about the risk-taking behavior of your teenage son, and nothing will interfere with your ability to show him your love. Drop your concern over a pending surgery, and you will continue enjoying each moment of your life in the meantime—and deal with the surgery when it becomes a reality instead of for weeks before.

Animals are beautiful mirrors for how we can respond to life without holding on to drama. My aged Bishon Frise was showing signs of declining health through a weakened immune system, which made him vulnerable to numerous infections. He had benign but itchy polyps all over his body, high blood pressure, and pressure on his bronchia that caused sporadic lengthy bouts of coughing. When coughing and gasping for air, all the while his tail was wagging as he looked at me lovingly. In his simple animal nature, he didn't identify with his illness, as if it defined him. He didn't create a drama around it. Maintaining his sweet doggie devotion, he continued to express the joy of simply being alive.

Assumptions Feed Drama

A MORE SUBTLE WAY we create drama is through making assumptions. Such assumptions are a disguised form of judgment. These often become the basis of intentional gossip.

We can so easily fall into assuming. The phone rings, and as we are walking to answer it, the chatter starts up in our mind. Who could be calling, and why? An unexpected package arrives in the mail. Automatically we scan our memory bank, making an assumption about who it's from and what it contains.

When we are present, we don't make assumptions. We simply go to the phone and pick it up to find out who is calling. Or we open the package and see what it is. In this way we drop the drama and instead live in the fresh and vibrant present moment.

We create a lot of drama in our lives by dwelling on possible "fearful" aspects of life—the trials that will come with inevitable aging, things that might go wrong to prevent the holiday from going smoothly, or the consequences of a downturn in the stock market. You can put yourself in a state of paranoia without any basis whatsoever for your fears just by making assumptions.

Let me share with you an account told to me a few years ago. A friend was heading into a neighborhood grocery store and noticed a young panhandler sitting on the pavement. The scene touched her heart. "He is someone's beloved son," she told herself. While shopping, she picked up a gourmet chocolate chip cookie to give him on her way out.

Leaving the store, my friend leaned down to hand the cookie to the panhandler. She was surprised when, instead of taking it immediately, he asked, "Does it have chocolate in it?"

"Yes, it does," she confirmed.

"Then, no thank you," said the young lad.

My friend conveyed to me how put off she was by this youngster. Here he was on the street, supposedly hungry, yet he could turn down her generous offering. Hmpf!

A few weeks later, shopping at the same grocery store, my friend found that she was still incensed by the incident of the panhandler. At the checkout, she related the story to the clerk.

"Oh," said the clerk, "his name is Ivan. He is highly allergic to chocolate."

My friend collapsed inside with shame for assuming Ivan was being picky. Surely all of us can recount times when we too made assumptions that proved to be untrue.

Any psychologist or conflict resolution professional will tell you how much pain is caused by individuals making baseless assumptions and then acting on them as if they were true.

Assumptions are born out of our inability to live with uncertainty. So we fabricate things in our mind to answer the small and larger unknowns we encounter in life. We want to know, to be certain. This is born out of egoic fear, which creates a need to be safe in the world. When we drop the ego with its concomitant fear, we will be able to be in the present moment, coming from direct experience, and be more than satisfied with this.

∿ *Projection Feeds Drama*

WHEN WE SEE AN ACTOR in a movie, we project all kinds of character traits onto this person in real life. Even though we don't know them, we imagine how they might be. The movie *The Queen* perfectly conveys how we also do this with public figures, as one of the characters remarks that the Queen is someone we think we all know, though none of us really know her at all.

In our everyday lives, we do the same with the people around us. Perceiving ourselves to be separate from others, we project roles onto them as if this is who they are. When we project, life's passing scenes then take on the appearance of a drama. This happens because projections feed our victim and victor roles, and the struggle that ensues between them. As long as we are projecting our own internal issues onto others, we cannot be at peace with ourselves.

Before we can correct our perceptions and end the drama, we first need to own these projections. Suppose something distresses you. You would not be in distress were projection not occurring. Whenever you are experiencing anything less than peace between yourself and another person, projection is always taking place. Instead of seeing the person as they really are, you are putting your own negativity onto them—projecting an aspect of yourself "out there," instead of facing up to it within yourself.

We can see people as they are—recognizing their flaws—without judging. This is perfectly all right, as long as we are at peace. There is only a problem when what we see upsets us—a sure sign that projection is taking place.

When another person distresses us and we go into reactivity, it is because we have projected onto that person some aspect of ourselves that we do not want to see. At such times, it is important to go into stillness and ask our inner knower what we are not seeing about ourselves that is causing us to react to the person and not experience peace. Our inner knower will then correct our perception of both ourselves and the other.

Where there is no projection, there is no fear. Where there is no fear, there is no separation. Where there is no separation, there is peace. When you see with your spiritual eyes, you see the divine everywhere and in everyone, and hence experience only peace.

Most fear emanates from thought. Our mind has been conditioned by the past, so it automatically makes judgments in the present based on previous experiences. These judgments are projected outward onto others. We then react to our projections, not to how the person really is, and so only get further away from the reality of the other person. We do the same thing with situations and events.

If you drop judgment, and just be present in life, what do you really see when you look at another person or a situation? What do you actually experience about them? When you encounter the real person or experience the situation, free of your fearful projections, life becomes far less dramatic. Indeed, living is so simple when it is not complicated by the projections of the mind.

From Participating to Witnessing

WHEN WE BLINDLY participate in drama, meaning when we *become* the protagonist in our own drama or a supporting role in someone else's, we lose ourselves in that role. We are then no longer conscious that we are playing a part. When this happens, we can't access anything outside the drama to break out of this illusion. As the protagonist or member of the supporting cast, we become the victim of illusion.

To help us break out of our dramas, many spiritual traditions advise that we cultivate the practice of self-observation or of witnessing ourselves. This requires a deliberate intention to break free from identification with our dramatic roles. By becoming a witness to the roles we play, we break identification with these roles and bring in another level of awareness.

When we witness ourselves, we come to see that there are at least two levels of consciousness—identification with the role, and watcher of the player of the role. From the position of a witness, we can see things that we are blind to when we are fully identified with our role. We can then better see ourselves as others see us. We can observe our dysfunctional ego at work. We can identify motives we keep hidden from ourselves when we play our roles. Witnessing ourselves is powerful because through it we start to experience that we are not who we think we are. We are not our egoic self but infinitely more than that.

The perception shifts that come with being able to witness yourself are from "I am only this" to "I am more than this." From "I am just my body" to "I am more than my body." From "I believe human drama is important" to "This is not important."

Is there something beyond the witnessing state? Yes. This is the state of pure *being*. The shift is from identification with the observer to the realization that you are the expression of the divine. This new state of Self-awareness is a shift from identification with separation and the feeling, "I am alone," to a realization of oneness and a sense of, "I am not alone." It is a movement from observing life, to realizing you are not separate from life—you *are* life.

When you experience drama in your personal life, do you feed it and keep it going? When you begin to witness your own drama, you are able to bring to this illusory form of life the essence of your divine Self. When you witness yourself being selfish, you are then free to choose to be generous. When you witness yourself reacting to your children in anger, you can choose to be peaceful in that situation. When you are falsely accused by your neighbor, instead of reacting to the false accusation, you can stand your ground in stillness and peace, bringing an end to the drama—at least for yourself. When you notice that you have thrown yourself into the pit of martyrs, you can correct your perception and remind yourself that as a divine being, you cannot be a victim of anyone or any circumstance. In this way, you can break free from the lure of the victim and victor roles that perpetuate your dramas.

When you see your sisters and brothers caught up in their dramas, you can assist them to break out of them by not entering them yourself. Be the silent witness to their dramas. Don't buy into their sad stories. Sympathy is demeaning, not redeeming. Don't participate in or encourage their storytelling or gossip.

Most of what we read in the newspaper and see on the television news is drama, much of it on a collective scale. Note the same perpetrator, victim, and victor roles being played. As a society, we are so hungry for drama on both the personal and collective levels that we may blindly perpetuate it against our best interests on both levels. We have become so addicted to drama that we seem to want it to continue even when it becomes dangerous to us. The combination of this addiction and our modern technologies could cause us to trigger a nightmare on our planet simply from a lack of awareness that we have pushed things beyond any semblance of sanity and control.

When reading events in the newspaper or watching them unfold on television, note the facts but don't enter into the drama. Feel the appropriate response to the situation. See the event for what it is, but don't get caught up in the human drama. Remind yourself that beneath all drama, you can find the reality of inner peace.

CHAPTER FIVE

Be-*ing Your Divine Self*

S PIRITUAL DISCIPLINES AND RELIGIONS have generally impressed upon us that we need to seek God in
order to find God. This idea of needing to take a
"journey" to find the divine originates in the fact that we have been led
to believe God is separate from us.

We have been conditioned to pray to a God outside us, when in fact
we are one with God. Because we don't see the obvious, we go on a long
journey in search of our divine Self. We think it requires myriad steps
and numerous lessons learned before we can claim our divinity. We tell
ourselves there is still so much more that we need to learn before we can
claim divine realization.

This is like searching outside of yourself, in the world around you,
to find yourself, when all the while you are the self for which you are

searching. In other words, we have been looking away to the horizon to try to find our true Self, when it can only be found on the holy ground upon which we presently stand.

The spiritual "journey" so many of us engage in isn't actually a journey at all. It's merely going around and around in our egoic mind. The drama of this search fuels the ego. It has rightly been said, "The ego's dictum is seek and do not find."[7] The ego doesn't want to find God because by doing so it knows it will be replaced by the true self. Indeed, our search for God will be never-ending as long as it is a search conducted by our egoic self.

The losing of an identity based in ego, and the emergence of a sense of identity rooted in our universal divine Self, requires no agonizing struggle. In fact, to enter into any kind of struggle to "find" God in our lives is self-defeating.

There *is* a journey to be taken, but it is not a journey to find God. It involves walking with God, not toward God. Indeed, it is God walking the Earth *as* us.

What Is Enlightenment?

I NOTICED A PLAQUE IN A CURIO shop and laughed upon reading the message. It said, "I wish I could be the person my dog thinks I am." If you have a dog, you have experienced its blessed unconditional love and ever-present adoring glances.

The good news is that you already *are* the person your dog thinks you are, but you just don't believe it. *Enlightenment is the experience of finally recognizing for yourself what your dog has known about you all along.* Animals play an important role in the evolution of human consciousness. So if you have a dog, let it be a constant reminder to you of your utter lovability.

At first, you may have a hard time believing that you are the wonderful person your dog knows you to be. Your beliefs about yourself are most likely blocking your ability to see the truth about yourself. Beliefs, being mind-based, usually stand in the way of truth.

Consider some of the beliefs that everyone once held, all of which proved to be untrue. At one time we believed the world was flat, but it is not so. We believed the earth was the center of our solar system, but it is not so. We believed humans would never take to the air, but it is not so. Today, most of us believe we are separate, vulnerable, flawed beings, but this too is not so. In a similar way, we may believe we are nothing more than advanced animals, but such a belief does not negate the truth of our divine nature. Regardless of what we believe about ourselves, we are who we are. We are the universal Presence, being itself.

∿ Agreements

THROUGHOUT OUR LIVES WE MAKE agreements, and our life experiences usually reflect these agreements. If you agree that life will be hard, it probably will be. If you agree that the number 13 is unlucky, for you it may well be unlucky. If you agree that Hawaii is the best place to vacation, for you this is where you will experience the greatest relaxation. If you agree that your Mary is the best wife in the world, you will no doubt be happy in your marriage.

Our experience of life reflects our agreements, and our agreements reflect how we see ourselves. In other words, what we agree to in life reflects our self-concept, our self-image. Coming from our shallow egoic self-image, most of our agreements are superficial, entered into with little if any real consciousness.

Since our agreements are personal and relative, they can be changed if we choose to change them. Tomorrow or next year, you could decide that 13 is actually a lucky number, that Europe is the best place to vacation, and that Susan is the best wife for you. In other words, many of your agreements with life have no deeper roots than what you choose to experience at any point in time.

The Leap asks us to change our *fundamental* agreement with life. This change can only come from a deep awareness of ourselves—far deeper than the images we carry of ourselves. To make such an important change involves changing how we perceive our *nature*.

The leap we are being invited to take involves making an agreement to accept and live from divine consciousness. It is a leap from living according to our misperceived limited human nature, to living according to our absolute, unchanging divine nature. In other words, it is a leap from ignorance and illusion into reality.

Our divine Self, unlike our relative and changing experiences based on our other agreements with life, does not change. It cannot, because it is who we are. It only awaits our agreement with it. When we make such an agreement, it becomes the basis of our entire life experience. This is how Jesus and the Buddha functioned. This is what any spiritual master does.

⌒ Get a Real Life

NO DOUBT YOU WANT TO experience love and peace and joy. To accomplish this, you feel you need to change yourself and your life experiences—to make yourself and your life "better" in some way. This striving is in vain because it is based on two errors.

The first error is thinking that you are not already exactly the person you seek to be. You *are* this person—you just haven't recognized it.

There is a difference between who you *intrinsically* are, and what you have so far experienced yourself to be. Just because you have not yet been able to experience the fullness of your true self, this doesn't mean that in fact you are not already whole.

The second error is imagining you can find happiness outside of yourself. "Get a life," people often say. They usually mean find friends and activities to occupy you in your external life. I want to say, "Get an *inner* life." Your inner life is the source of a *real* life. It is so much more exciting than anything you can draw to yourself from outside of yourself.

You don't need to change yourself or achieve something in order to experience love and peace and joy, because these are characteristics of your true nature. They form the signature of your being.

Consider love, for instance. When you feel deep love for your child, where *is* the love? It is not in the child. It is inside you. The child simply evokes your love and becomes its recipient.

The same is true of every wonderful aspect of life. When you are moved by the beauty of a sunset, it is your own inner beauty finding expression and being mirrored back to you. When you experience an uncaused wellspring of joy, it is your own true being pressing through and finding expression.

In each of these cases, it is *you* who is the love, the beauty, the joy. This is your true self, hidden beneath the false perceptions of yourself that you have been conditioned to believe in.

For a moment, just think about the misperceptions we have of ourselves. Most of us live in perpetual dislike of different elements of ourselves. We are plagued by self-doubt, which causes us to second-guess ourselves all the time. We are forever looking over our shoulder, wondering if we are doing the right thing. Instead of living confidently, calmly, serenely, we are often drenched in anxiety about how people see us, whether they accept us, whether they think highly of us.

Did it ever occur to you that by not accepting yourself as you are, you actively deny who you really are? *Trying to change yourself is a means of actively denying your true self.*

Accepting yourself as you are, with all your gifts, characteristics, fears, habits, and desires opens the door to self-love. You don't need time, instructions, guidelines, techniques, or self-examination in order to enjoy self-love.

When people seek to change themselves, they are usually banking on their ability to perfect their egoic self. In other words, they are putting faith in their *false* self to bring them the happiness they seek. Notice the expressions we associate with such change—self-improvement, personal growth, becoming more "spiritual." These are activities of the ego seeking to bolster itself. By engaging in them, we reinforce our belief in the false self and thereby make it difficult for our true nature to find expression.

Living from your true being would, of course, bring death to the ego. It is therefore not surprising that the ego is ready to put up a mighty and ongoing fight to convince you that it is the "real" you. Thanks to the work of authors such as Eckhart Tolle, for the first time in human history the ego is now fighting for its very existence. However, we must not be seduced by the ego into entering this fight. To fight the ego is to use its own sword of fear on ourselves. To fight the ego is to strengthen it by giving attention to it. Part of what is involved in making the Leap is to go beyond the ego, to leave it behind. The surest way to go beyond ego is simply to live from your divine Self. It's the same as getting rid of darkness—you don't fight the darkness, you just flip on the light switch. In the same way, you oust the ego by embracing and living as your magnificent true Self.

When you accept yourself as you are now, you are more able to accept your life as it is now. When you do this, you realize that feeling joy, peace, or inner stillness is not dependent on what happens in your life. You realize that you cannot create good feelings by changing your situation or changing other people. Feeling joy is not dependent on external factors. When you experience uncaused joy and inexplicable peace even in times of crisis, you will then know that you are free of the influence of the world.

By dropping self-judgment, and instead loving all of yourself as you are right now—loving the seeming weaknesses as well as the strengths—you create a space for your true self to shine through. Jesus told us, "Be ye therefore perfect, even as your Father which is in heaven is perfect." [8] In telling us to be "perfect," Jesus was not trying to extract an impossible behavioral standard from us. He wasn't dooming us to a life of utter frustration, as we struggle to be something we are incapable of being. Rather, he was expressing the truth of our being and reminding us of who we really are.

The way to *experience* the truth about ourselves is to bring love to everything about ourselves. Said the Jewish philosopher Martin Buber, there is nothing that cannot be made sacred. Another way of saying this is that there is nothing that is not already sacred. We only need to recognize the sacredness in everything, including ourselves. At every stage in the evolutionary process, all is sacred, because it has all led up to this point where we are now able to take this leap in consciousness.

Living Our Divinity

IF OUR VERY BEING IS DIVINE, how could we have missed seeing this for so long? Is it *because* it is so obvious that it is hard for us to see? Said Henry David Thoreau, "The light that puts out our eyes is blindness to us." Most of us have experienced this when driving our car into direct sunlight, particularly when the sun has just risen above the horizon or is sinking low in the sky toward sunset. We cannot see simply because the light *is* so bright. The very sunlight that enables us to see blinds us.

So how do we recover our vision when we are being blinded by the light? The answer is that we don't need the kind of vision that *looks at* things. You and I are being asked to take a leap into a whole new way of experiencing ourselves. We are being asked to embrace our divine Self by *be*-ing this divine Self. We simply need to *be* the light that we already are. Then there are no observing eyes to be blinded.

We speak of ourselves as human beings. For most of us, this conjures up an image of a fixed entity. In other words, we regard "being" as a noun. People imagine they are simply what they are—what their genes and upbringing made them, end of story.

If our being is a fixed entity, then any fulfillment we hope for in our personal lives or as a species will be limited by what has been handed to us. We may tinker with aspects of our behavior, but we really can't expect too much.

When people do seek inner change, often they speak of "becoming my true self" or "realizing my true being." It's as if becoming our true self or realizing our being was a fixed state to be achieved. "Being" is envisioned as a once-and-for-all entry into a kind of cocoon in which we experience a peaceful condition where everything is light and love. The "joy of being" is then viewed as a static and permanent state of bliss.

Realizing our true being is also something we tend to hope will happen to us someday. But we can't imagine it happening today. We tell ourselves that if we strive for it hard enough and meditate a great deal, we will eventually "arrive." For most of us, it isn't a now experience—not something we can *be this very minute.*

The Leap involves a correction in perception. Being is a verb, and the realization of our being is very much an active state. Instead of an inert condition to be entered into, *being* involves a *felt* "aliveness" that fuels a way of living in the world—a way of "doing life."

Sometimes we hear folk say, "We are all God." It sounds like they are claiming ultimate status. But did you ever think of God not as a noun, but as an "ing" *verb?*

My divine Self isn't a status I hold—it is something I am *be-*ing. The "realization" of my being involves experiencing my oneness with divine Source in all of its glorious, harmonious, and unbounded self-expression. Consequently, far from being a static existence, a spiritual life is one that expands and extends itself without limit. I am *be-*ing my divine Self when I *live* the attributes of my divinity.

God is consciousness. This consciousness is stillness, an emptiness that is void of "things." Yet, even though this consciousness is an emptiness of form, it is vibrantly active, ever-expressing, resulting in the creation of endless forms. Indeed, this nothingness ("no-thingness") is the womb of the Big Bang and the teeming life forms that have arisen from this creative event.

The spiritual journey isn't toward a destination somewhere outside of ourselves. Neither is it a journey within ourselves. Both are common misconceptions of spirituality. Instead, the spiritual journey involves becoming aware of our divine Self *by actively extending our divine Self into all that we say and do.*

In other words, attributes such as peace, joy, and love, which are characteristic of our divinity, are not something we possess—not fixed attributes. They are *energy.* They flow from the no-thingness that is our divine Self. They are the outpouring of an energy that is the very essence of our makeup. We find joy in *be*-ing divine.

I am *being* peace when I imbue all that I think, say, and do with a peaceful energy. I am *being* joy by bringing this energy into all my experiences. I am *being* love by expressing love in all of my thoughts, words, and actions.

Once you access your inner life, you will discover a reservoir of infinite potential. Out of a flow of peace, joy, and love, you will continually make fresh discoveries, embark on exciting adventures, and engage in boundless creativity.

This vision of a spiritual person is drastically different from the image of spirituality that has dominated for centuries. Spirituality has for many been linked with avoidance of a deep involvement in the world. Our spiritual practices have normally taken place in a formal church setting or when we take "time out" from the world. But spiritual practices need to lead to implementing our divine attributes in the situations we face as we live our everyday lives.

You may ask, "Well then, what about the contemplative life? Isn't this an important vocation?" It can indeed be. Spiritual contemplatives who live a hermetic life often have a rich inner experience of their divine Self that imbues them with a radiance reflecting an authentic spiritual power. Consequently, their normally invisible actions, however modest in worldly terms, have a redemptive effect on all of us, as do their prayers. Indeed, people who live a life of contemplation usually do so *because* they feel this is how they can best contribute to the world. There is nothing small or self-centered about the life of such contemplatives.

∼ Own, Share, Then Be Your Divine Self

W HEN YOU FEEL A WARM PEACE envelop you in the early dawn, do you imagine that such a peace just materializes out of nowhere? We have already seen that it doesn't. It comes from deep within your self. You *are* that peace.

When you think of your child, and an overwhelming love for her washes over you, we have already seen that this love is who you are. This love isn't something you have to "try" to muster—it's just *there*.

Whenever you find yourself spontaneously expressing any of your divine qualities, you are being who you *really* are—you are *being God* in the world. As your divine attributes manifest as actions, divine love flows into the cosmos.

I had my first brief experience of *being* love several years ago. My husband and I were on a short vacation not far from our home city of Vancouver, Canada. In keeping with our need for rest and replenishment, we both booked massages for the same hour. We were right next to each other, divided only by a curtain. As I was relaxing into the gentle touch of the therapist, I was hoping that my husband was able to relax and enjoy his treatment as much as I was enjoying mine. I then purposely sent him my love. No sooner had I begun to do this than I experienced a dramatic shift in consciousness. I was not merely sending my husband love, I *was* the love! In that instant, I knew what it meant to love as God loves. Every cell of my being was *actively* sending love. The love energy was so full, so ecstatic. It extended so completely and palpably throughout my body and outward into the entire universe. I felt myself no longer to be a limited individual, but had burst into an endless energy of sublime love that contained yet went beyond all that is.

Soon, however, the fear-based ego crept in, telling me it was just *too much* love to bear in my bodily frame without being engulfed by it to the point I would disappear altogether. As soon as I decided that it was too beautiful to bear, the intensity of the love energy began to wane. In a minute or so, I was back to simply "human mode." But that one experience of truly *being* love changed my awareness and my life.

This incident supports something Marianne Williamson once said—that it is not our darkness we fear most, but our light. We are afraid of the power of our own light—terrified of experiencing our own utter beauty as incarnations of the divine. Why have we become so afraid of our light? Only because we have become so familiar with the illusion of our egoic self. We are like children who would rather hang onto the false security found in familiar pain from abusive parents than to risk losing them.

Why, at times, are we so naturally our divine Self, whereas at other times it seems extremely difficult? It is because we have been conditioned to see ourselves as separate from and less than our divine Self. Over eons of time, humanity has become encrusted in this conditioning, each generation reinforcing it and passing it on to the next. But beneath this encrusted outer shell is our true Self.

Every now and then in history, there have been those who break through the encrustation of conditioning to see the truth of their being. They bring light to others, often triggering great change in them, and even in the human condition as a whole. The ability of such individuals to realize they are divine serves as a sweet reminder to all of us of who we really are.

It is now time for the "critical mass" of humanity to claim this same awareness. The survival of our species on this planet depends on it. You and I are a vital part of the emergence of the new consciousness. May we express our divine essence just as freely and easily as a flower expresses its flower essence, extending its beauty and spreading its fragrance to all who will receive it. The flower has no difficulty being itself—neither does the leaf, the tree, the cat, the lion. They are each doing what comes naturally to them.

Would you like to see peace in the world? Then *be* an expression of peace. When you say to another "Peace be with you," don't just express it as a wish or a blessing, but inwardly know that it is a fact. You could also boldly tell them, "Peace is with you, *as* you." You would thereby provide the person with sweet remembrance and encourage their true state to emerge. First claim your peace, then *be* the peace by bringing peace into each of your relationships. When you are being peaceful, you have no enemies, no one you hold things against, and no desire for revenge. You do not put others down or attack them because they oppose you. You relate to everyone peaceably.

You are here to wake up to your divinity, to own your divine attributes, and to share them with everyone.

⁓ Spiritual Integrity

WE ALL WANT TO DO worthwhile things so that we have a positive influence in the world. But Mahatma Gandhi emphasized putting being and doing in the correct order. "First *be* the truth you want to see in others," he said.

At one point in his life, Gandhi agreed to set aside certain times during the week when he would receive people. On one such occasion, a woman and her son were brought to him. The woman was distressed and explained to Gandhi that her son was making himself sick by eating too much candy. No matter what she said or what discipline she applied, her son continued to eat abundant amounts of sweets. "Mahatma, Mahatma, please tell him not to eat sweets," she pleaded. "He will listen to you. Please, Mahatma, please."

Gandhi looked at the boy, then back at the mother, then once again at the boy. Turning back to the mother, he responded, "Please come back with your son in three days."

The mother left with her son, and both returned at the appointed time. When they were ushered in to see him, Gandhi stood up to greet them, then walked straight to within a few feet of the boy. To emphasize his words, Gandhi raised his right hand and pointed his index finger, then said slowly to the boy in a calm but serious tone, "Don't eat sweets."

The mother quickly piped up. "What, Mahatma? That is all you have to say? Why didn't you tell my son this three days ago?"

Without hesitation Gandhi answered, "Because three days ago, I was still eating sweets."

Gandhi was showing us that to be a teacher of spiritual truth, we first need to embody the teaching. In other words, we *are* the teaching. We have to be people of integrity who embody what we teach, otherwise we will be ineffective.

In this respect Mahatma Gandhi reminds us of the poor Parson in the Prologue to Geoffery Chaucer's *Canterbury Tales*. Of all the so-called religious people in The Prologue who served in positions of the organized church, the poor Parson, a humble parish priest, was the only one who was authentically spiritual. Chaucer tells us the Parson not only practiced what he preached, but practiced *before* he preached.

"If gold rusts, what will iron do?" asked the Parson. If we who purport to know better cannot practice the truth we mouth, how can we expect others who don't know any better to practice it?

This is why the contents of some spiritual books have real transformative power, whereas others do not. Transformative books emerge from the authentic state of being that they are trying to bring to the awareness of their readers. As such, a transference takes place, as the writer's Presence is carried through the words and extended to the reader, thereby awakening the reader to their own Presence.

When we are anchored in our true being, we are in a state of Presence. Presence is not only powerful but also contagious. It is magnetic, evoking the Presence in others, whether they are already conscious of their inner Presence or not.

Mahatma Gandhi knew that his instruction not to eat sweets would fall on barren soil unless he was already living this himself. We too need to know that the power we have to effect positive change and healing in our world comes from practicing before we preach.

To bring peace into a situation, we first have to be at peace ourselves. We must embody the qualities of tolerance, non-judgment, acceptance, and respect that we want to see in the world. For example, to foster the dissolution of terrorism, we first need to stop our own attack thoughts and strategies—in all their varied and often subtle forms.

CHAPTER SIX

Divine Love

*I*F YOU WANT TO START EXPERIENCING your divine nature, don't go to the past to figure out how to live in the present. The past holds only the story of your false self. Thinking back to the past, looking to it for guidance, serves only to lock you into your story, closing the door to your divine Self which is experienced only in the present.

You can never express your divine Self and all of its attributes such as love, joy, and peace in the past. If it is important for your spiritual evolution to remember something from the past, it will come to you in the present, at the precise moment you need it.

If you want to experience your divine nature, don't escape to the future either, as the future is nothing but wishful thinking or fearful projection, both still based on your past conditioning.

You Are Much More
Than You Think You Are

I HAVE HAD THE PRIVILEGE OF working with two enlightened authors. In both instances, their enlightenment came through a sudden experience of disidentification with the ego. Once the false self fell away, their true divine Self just took over.

Suddenly becoming enlightened is not the experience of most of us. We can either wait for this rare occurrence to happen to us too, or we can shake ourselves awake by expressing the divine love we already are. As it has been said, "Teach only love, for that is what you are."[9]

How can you recognize that you are only love? By extending love to all, all of the time. It is only by giving love that you come to the realization that you *are* the love you are giving.

As you practice being loving, you will find yourself becoming more buoyant and feeling more "alive," because you cannot extend the love that you are without this healing and elevating energy coming back to you. When it does, it reminds you that you can't really give anything away because you are the source of love. So all giving is really to ourselves!

Everything simply works when we live from our divine Self. As we extend love, our body produces more endorphins, which bring about a heightened sense of wellbeing. As we continue to practice living from our divine nature, it feels so good to be who we truly are that we no longer want to do anything to diminish this feeling. Once we start living from our true nature, any lapse that takes us back to the false egoic self with its fear-driven behavior only serves to underscore that we are *not* that.

⟨⟩ *What Does Divine Love Look Like?*

*H*OW WOULD WE LOVE if we were not impeded by the ego? How would we love if we loved like the divine Self we really are?

Have you ever been in a room when someone entered and immediately you could feel their Presence? Some people simply radiate calmness, joy, enthusiasm, confidence. You can literally feel these qualities.

When we love like the divine Self we really are, we become such fields of Presence, exuding divine attributes. We will express these divine attributes in varying intensity according to our unique makeup.

Even though there will be differences in the degree to which various attributes of the divine are manifested through us—some of us more enthusiastic, some of us more quietly confident—all of us will radiate love, extending it effortlessly and in the fullness of joy to all of life. We will love because that is what we do in our divinity. Our divine Self loves to extend itself, and holds only gratitude for opportunities to do so.

The hallmark of divine love is that it is devoid of fear. In the absence of fear, there is nothing to impede the flow of our love. This is why divine love can only be extended by our divine Self, not the egoic self which grew out of and is sustained by fear. It is also why many spiritual teachers tell us to resist nothing, and to surrender to what is. In order to do this, we need to drop fear. By doing so, we open the way for love to flow into all our experiences, and beyond us into our world.

Divine love has no choice but to extend itself. It is universally inclusive and unconditional. It doesn't require anything of the objects of its love. Since it goes beyond personal love, it takes nothing personally and therefore cannot be slighted. Divine love is not limited by the boundaries of what we call time. It is eternally given. It is never disturbed because it sees only the reality of love in all persons and situations. It is without judgment. Divine love doesn't need to wait until someone is "sinless" before it gives of itself to them. It unconditionally accepts all—all people and all situations as they are right now.

At the visceral level, when we love with divine love, there is a softening of our perceptions and a softening of the way we experience being in the body.

The sure test of whether you are loving with divine love is to ask if there is any fear in this love. When I love my wife, is this love free of fear? When I love my children, is my love given without fear?

Most, if not all, of us would say that we love God. But many of us have been brought up to fear God. How can one fear that which is only love? To equate fear with God is an oxymoron, yet it is one most of us have lived with all our lives. Fear by its very nature leads to the illusion so many of us hold that we are separate from God. We cut ourselves off from our divine nature because of this fear.

Do you love your life? Many have a love-hate relationship with their lives. Their enjoyment of life is undercut by a deep distrust—a sense that the proverbial "other shoe" is about to drop.

For example, I got into an elevator, and a maintenance man with a bucket entered. He immediately struck up a conversation by asking, "How are you today?"

"I'm just wonderful!" I enthused.

"Oh, I'd never say that," the maintenance man responded. "I'd be afraid that if I let myself feel that good, I'd have to pay for it later. I prefer to stay in the groove."

What a pity! This kind man was cutting himself off from the joy of life because of his belief that life can't be trusted to bring him only good things.

The maintenance man isn't alone in feeling a distrust of life. I have noticed that whenever a person says they feel wonderful and really means it, people look at them like they must be fibbing. Why? Because such people have never allowed themselves to experience with abandonment the joy of life.

When we don't believe that love is the basis of everything, we don't trust life to be absolutely supportive, benign, and giving to us, and therefore we fear life.

People also tend to be afraid of other people's pain. When we run from being with others in their pain, we are not coming from divine love, but from fear of vicariously experiencing the pain of the other. Mother Mary did not run from the foot of the cross. Can we as parents claim to love our children in a way that we don't run from or enter into fear when they experience acute pain in their lives? Can we trust in their inner wisdom, and the wisdom of life itself, even when they go against our wishes or stray from our personal values?

All of the apostles save John ran from the foot of the cross. They ran and hid after Jesus' death for fear of being associated with him, of being identified as his disciples and thereby becoming targets for the same untimely end. They hid in an upper annex, huddling together until they were visited by the essence of the resurrected Christ and then experienced the descent of the Holy Spirit. It was only after they were filled with the spirit—a realization of their divine nature—that they left the annex and ran into the streets to dance with jubilation, letting all see their exuberance. In accepting that they too were divine like Jesus, all fear left them. There is no room for fear when you accept your divinity. Then, and only then, were the disciples prepared to go forth and bring the teaching of Jesus to the world.

When dying on the cross, Jesus forgave his torturers and executioners. He could forgive because he was total love and therefore devoid of all fear. He had no fear of further pain, of death of the body, and least of all of the one he called his heavenly Father. So it was that he could say, as his last words, "Into your hands I commend my spirit."[10]

The gift of Jesus' imminent death is in the *way* he responded to his death, which serves as a clear statement to us of what divine love is. In this light, we are all on a journey to the cross. We are challenged to express divine love in all we do and at all times, even when human anger and self-pity seem justified.

Let us go to the cross, where the human meets the divine in ourselves and the divine is all that shines forth. And let us do it now, before we die physically. If we don't, we will once again miss realizing our human purpose, which is to bring divine love into this human condition and thereby come to recognize the divine Self we truly are.

Compassion Trumps Sympathy

RECALL THE OCCASION on which Mother Teresa found a newborn infant in a Calcutta gutter. There was no pity in her eyes as she gazed at this infant, only adoring love, flowing from the recognition of the perfect being she was holding in the palm of her hand. Mother Teresa had made the leap from human sympathy to divine compassion. She looked at the tiny babe with eyes filled with divine compassion, and the babe responded from the divine life incarnate in it.

When we come from human sympathy, we regret that things are as they are, wishing they were otherwise, and thus reinforce imperfection. When we come from divine compassion, we see through the seeming negative to a person's divine Self. No matter how bad things appear, we know that ultimately all is well. Taking this approach, we reinforce our own awareness of our divinity and bring about a remembrance of the divinity in others.

Divine compassion is an affirmation of the mighty Presence every-where in all situations and all creatures, at all times. The divine Self we are has noble eyes. It can only see love everywhere, or love emerging everywhere.

⟳ Divine Love Has Many Forms of Expression

*D*IVINE LOVE IS NOT ALWAYS EXPRESSED in a soft and warm manner, however. Sometimes it is boldly expressed and may initially be experienced as aggressive. Witness Jesus driving out the moneylenders in the temple. It has been said that his rebuke was fierce. There is room for rebuke if it is loving rebuke.

A Zen story illustrates this beautifully. A Zen master took his three students to the city for a break from their intense study and practices. That day, he suggested his students go into town to shop and enjoy the sights of the market place. The students responded with delight to this suggestion and quickly headed off. Since the market was a distance away, they decided to take a rickshaw. Upon climbing into the rickshaw, the female student was attacked by a thief who wrestled with her for her purse. That evening after supper, the Zen master asked his students how they enjoyed their day in town. The female student told of how her purse was stolen from her. The master listened with great attention. When the girl had concluded the story, the master said, "Oh, my dear, why didn't you, *with the most loving kindness in your heart*, hit the thief over the head with your umbrella?"

The Zen Master was teaching his students that we need to go to our heart first to assess the most appropriate, most loving response, then take action. A plea of, "Please don't steal my purse," would have fallen on deaf ears, as would saying, "Please don't take this. It contains the only money I have to buy a present for my master." The Zen master knew that this situation called for a sharp physical rebuke—a loving but hard knock to stop the thief! Such a response is an act of love—not because it might save the purse to buy the present for the master, but because it might cause the thief to "listen up" in the only way he could at his level of consciousness.

It is up to us to discern how to most appropriately express our love in different situations. This means being open to the still small voice of our indwelling inner knower to guide us. Sometimes, words or actions will not be called for, just a silent blessing of the person or situation, or visualizing them being surrounded by healing white light.

You may ask, how can I extend divine love to someone who is about to attack me? The preceding Zen story gives us the clue. Suppose a burglar breaks into your house. What do you do? You try to stop him. It's your home, and he shouldn't have broken in. In defending yourself, however, make sure you do so from a place of love. If you come from love, your inner knower will guide you in what to do in the situation. By coming from love instead of reacting with anger, you minimize the repercussions. If you express hatred, this hatred will in some way come back to you.

When it comes to nations attacking each other, the tendency is to teach our armed forces to objectify the "enemy." But to defend ourselves, we don't need to turn others into inhuman objects. When we do this, we cannot see our common Self and can more easily deny the other person's value and thus act against them without conscience. Just as with the burglar, we can do what needs to be done from the most loving place in our heart. We take prudent and defensive action, but we don't buy into the hateful spirit from which the attacker may come.

In the martial arts, a contestant respects their opponent. This respect is an important aspect of achieving emotional balance. Contestants know that they must remain emotionally neutral if they are to have the inner balance that allows their core strength to come through. The Leap involves us going beyond even emotional neutrality, to actually loving our enemy. When forced to engage in self-defense, this is the way that we can emerge from the situation in a healthy spiritual state.

Do we always feel peaceful and warm when we love divinely? The picture of Christ Jesus dying on the cross, and the painting of the Sacred Heart of Jesus with open and bleeding heart, say no—as does the image of his stooped mother Mary at the foot of the cross cradling the body of her dead son.

Not to run from pain either in ourselves or in others, but to embrace it, is an act of divine love. It is perhaps during such times, when the heart physically seems to burn and break open with pain, that our love is most redemptive. We stand resolute in the pain, resisting nothing—not even focusing on hope that it will end. Our only purpose becomes to face the sadness, disaster, or tragedy and embrace it with the ultimate reality of love.

If you sit with your emotional pain and let it be, feeling fully the energy of this state, you will discover that there is something underneath it. Pain that is accepted, then embraced, begins to soften and break up. As it does so, a new state emerges that is still and peaceful. If you run from your pain, doing anything you can to avoid feeling it, you prevent yourself from experiencing the reality underneath it. Anyone who has fully surrendered themselves to grieving the loss of a loved one, even a beloved pet, will tell you that they had to feel the deep and excruciating pain of loss before they could come to the awareness that they could never really lose the other—that "Nothing real can be threatened."[11]

When we cannot accept, we create from a state of non-acceptance. If we run from our fear, we create out of fear. If we run from our pain, we create out of pain. Instead of resisting or running, if we accept these states, even embrace them, we are able to let go of the conditioned past from which they emanate. We can then heal and start anew.

～ Blessing Is a Divine Act

*J*UST AS COURTESY CAN BE the beginning of charity, so also blessing others can be the beginning of divine love. When we genuinely bless others, we extend egoless love. Through the work of Masaru Emoto, we have seen the power of blessing water. Blessing water can change the molecules from misshapen energy configurations to beautiful and symmetrical hexagonal crystal-like formations. If blessing water can have this effect, how much more transformational it will be when we bless each other!

You don't have to be a priest to bless water and make it holy. You can make it holy because *you* are holy. Bless and thereby transform everything in your world by acknowledging the divine in all things. Bless your enemy, bless your pet, bless the mail carrier, bless all who enter your home.

～ True Wealth—Our Divine Heritage

*W*E EACH HAVE WITHIN OUR HEARTS the means to create lives that exude a true richness, since love is the only real currency. We are deluded if we think that any artificial form of exchange, such as money, gold, precious stones, property, or valuable objects can produce anything of real value. This is why Jesus advised that we collect for ourselves "treasures in heaven, where neither moth nor rust destroys, and where thieves don't break in and destroy."[12] The only real treasures are those we acquire through loving.

Extending love pays abundant dividends. It is a universally desired commodity. Always in demand, its value never deteriorates. Neither can we exhaust our supply of love, because we *are* love.

Imagine the kind of world we would create if we all strove to be rich in love and measured our self-worth accordingly. Because we all have equal ability to express the love that we are, we could all be rich beyond measure. Based on the principle of "as within, so without," we would end our spiritual poverty and concurrently end world poverty.

CHAPTER SEVEN

The Push-Pull of Being Human

H UMANS ARE NATURALLY GREGARIOUS, valuing
community in many forms—family, friendships,
group experiences. We love to be close to others.
Physically, mentally, emotionally, and spiritually we long to touch others
and have them touch us.

Whenever there is authentic joining, no matter how briefly, all who
join benefit. When they separate to go their own way, they take some of
the positive energy of this communion with them. It happens in the
most ordinary of everyday events.

My husband and I attended a National Hockey League game. It was
a close, exciting game, and our hometown won. Leaving the stadium, we
were swept up in the crowd, walking twenty abreast and three blocks
deep. The enthusiastic fans were of course talking about the game. A
man to my husband's right made a comment to someone on his right,

saying he disagreed with the awarding of first star status for the game to a certain player. My husband too disagreed with this and made a comment to his neighbor on his right, endorsing his sentiment. This triggered an animated conversation. As the crowd thinned and it came time to part, I asked my husband who the man was. He said, "I don't know." I was surprised to hear this. Their exchange was so authentic that I assumed they must have known each other. It was a brief but sweet encounter of two hockey fans joining together with a common interest and point of view.

Notice how we come together with another with ease when we find something in common that we love, whether it be a love of a sport, of children, of a country, or of gardening. This also suggests what we must do at the collective level if we are going to go beyond our differences— find something that we value in common. It could be love of Mother Earth, of the feminine principle, of the children of the world, or of compassion for the oppressed. Is this not the answer my friend was seeking on his train commute home from New York City shortly after the attacks of 9/11?

Yes, fear can bring us together. But this togetherness is not sustained unless the cause of the fear continues. Will we always need a common enemy in order to rally together? Can we not go beyond connecting mostly in times of fear, or in victimhood, and connect in legitimate and lasting ways out of common love? And what could be more common than our own humanity, that "one big Self" the soldier at Guadalcanal was referring to? The time has never been more opportune for the leaders of the world to step forward to find and articulate the common ground that we have with other parties—and indeed as our "one big Self."

When individuals join together in love, an energy is released that is greater than the sum of the energy of the two. In moments of authentic joining, one plus one can equal, for instance, ten! Look at the exponential nature of joining sperm and ovum, seed and soil. This also occurs when groups form around a healthy intention, with each member pooling their strengths to accomplish what none could do alone.

At the same time, it also has to be recognized that some groups that consider themselves "support" groups actually detract from the experience of oneness. Based not in awareness of common Presence, but in neediness, members of such groups feel a kinship with each other that identifies them as victims. Victims always need an opposite. Instead of fostering a person's resilience, bringing out their strengths, such groups major in victimhood.

As we have seen, the egoic self believes it is separate from everyone else, which breeds fear. Such fear induces a victim or victor mentality, defensiveness, competition, and feelings of being better or worse than others in terms of one's circumstances, physical attributes, capabilities, and morals. This fear exists alongside the pull of love toward oneness. Indeed, the spiritual pull toward oneness is often used by the ego to set up group identities that serve to keep others out. We see this in such phenomena as tribalism, religious affiliation, politics, racism, and prejudice in all forms. Any togetherness that is ego-based is exclusive of others. The ego separates, while love joins. Community based on joining in love is always inclusive.

The pull toward oneness is in evidence everywhere. Life speaks to us frequently of our oneness, but do we have eyes to see and ears to hear? What you give your attention to tends to increase, so pay attention to the evidence of oneness in your life and note the increasing number of incidents that attest to it. Be alert to the times a mother intuitively knows her child is in danger, the times you want to say something and your partner says the exact same thing, the times you have a novel idea or inspirational breakthrough only to have your close friend or parent echo this back to you the next day. If you have a pet dog, you certainly know that dogs are aware of oneness. For example, they know when you are upset and need comforting—and they always seem to know when you are about to arrive home, either looking out the window or being at the front door to greet you.

Indeed, most synchronous and seemingly improbable coincidences are evidence of our oneness. Recall the afternoon you felt upset for no apparent reason, only to find out a day later that it was then that your dear friend was in a serious car accident. Notice how you can relate to and genuinely participate in the grief of another you have learned about through the newspaper or television. Sympathy pains give evidence of our oneness too. Feel how another can affect your energy body—how they replenish it, balance it, give it either a negative or positive charge.

In Greek mythology, Narcissus falls in love with his own image, which is reflected in a pool of water. He takes this image to be who he really is. This is what each of us does with respect to the ego. We believe the ego is real and fall in love with it. But this is not *real* self-love.

When you don't identify with your ego, you experience the reality of your inner Presence. Presence has no boundaries because it is the essence of all that is. Consequently, there is nothing individualistic about it. You cannot say, "This is my Presence, and that is your Presence," or, "I have more Presence than you." When you are in a state of Presence, your being experiences a vitality, and this is reflected in an aliveness that pervades your world. In such an aware state, you become attuned to the oneness of everything.

If you have had the privilege of sitting with a group of people in a state of shared Presence, you will likely have found your awareness of the individuals around you fading as the field of the one Presence becomes primary. The next time you experience this, note how wedded you feel with the other individuals, and they with you, from thereon after.

When you greet another from a state of Presence, you can instantly connect with the Presence in them. This is why when two conscious individuals meet each other for the first time, they readily engage in communion at a deep soul level. At such times, it is as if we are meeting our familiar self in the other. The person not only speaks *to* us but *for* us, and we for them. Keep this is mind when you are looking for a spiritual teacher, whether in book or bodily form. When you find a spiritual teacher who speaks *for* you, voicing what you intuit, you have found one of *your* teachers.

You Are Not Your Body

READING THE STORY OF Narcissus through the eyes of Presence, we see that he fell into the illusion that his physical form was his ultimate reality. But the external body and the external world are only passing forms, each of them transitory expressions of the ultimate reality.

When we identify with the ego, it causes us to see the body in a distorted way. Either we think the body is who we are, or we disdain our physicality and imagine ourselves a separate immortal soul housed in a body for a time. But our true self is neither the body nor an individualistic immortal soul. Rather, our true self is a part of the oneness of infinite Presence.

As a result of the distortion brought about by ego, the body becomes a partner with the ego in a conspiracy to keep us from the awareness of our true identity. We lose sight of our divinity altogether—especially of the fact that the body is itself an expression of divine consciousness.

We can never free ourselves from the illusion that we are our body by trying to escape the body. When we attempt such escape, we are like a prisoner who plans his escape from his cell, but who is always caught and returned to jail. As long as we identify with the role of prisoner of the ego, wearing the body as our identifiable prison garb, we will still be prisoners—albeit prisoners-on-the-run.

As our divine Self, we are already invulnerable and free. So the way to escape the ego is to replace it with awareness and acceptance of our divine Self.

We can repeatedly say, "I am not my body," but how can we actually come to know this if, while in this bodily frame, we cannot experience this? Words in themselves mean nothing. Unless they flow from the core of our being, they are powerless.

Our body screams out and says, I am hungry. I am cold. My nerves are acting up. My throat is sore today. I was in a car crash last year that left my right arm paralyzed. I am afraid of crowds. I grieve for my deceased brother. All of this seems so real.

On one level, of course, the body is real. It is a manifestation of consciousness. But it is not our ultimate reality. It is not who we are outside of time and form.

If we are going to become unstuck from our human tragedy, we will have to become unstuck not only from ego, but also from thinking our body is all we are—while simultaneously not derogating the body in any way. The body is vitally important to our awakening to consciousness. It is the form that enables us to have the experience of being human, and to use this experience to move toward awareness of our divinity. The body is our holy temple.

We do not *have* life, we *are* life. We participate in a universal reality, not a disconnected existence. We are part of an eternal oneness. As Jesus said, "I and my Father are one."[13] We and God are *also* one.

As the divine Self that I am, I am a co-creator of my world with God. I am one with God. By "God," I mean that which permeates everything.

There is nowhere God is not. There is no form that is not an expression of God.

When I am fully conscious of my divine Self, I can see only the light. I can experience only love and peace and joy. Going even deeper into the experience of my divine Self, I realize that I could never be a mere observer of life because I am in no way separate from life.

If we misidentify with the body as our only reality, we ensure that fear will be our predominant state, not love. What a brilliant way to keep the human drama going! The ego robs the human body of its true purpose—being a vehicle for the expression of divine love.

The ego will certainly be threatened by this awareness, but what if we now chose to end the game of "let's pretend dress up," unzipped our human body armor, stepped out of it, then discarded it? What would be left?

Well, we would have no need for food, clothing, and shelter—in short, no dependence on the external world for survival. We would have no means of comparing ourselves with others, either. Gone would be competition, vanity, blame, judgment—and their foundation, fear. Gone would be aggression and defensiveness, and the violent acts they spawn, since we would have no need to defend ourselves against others. There would be no need for elaborate and controlling structures and institutions, either. There would be no reason to worship anything in form outside of ourselves—including money, celebrities, powerful political figures, the forces of nature, or any other false god.

We would be left only with the awareness of our pure spiritual essence. We would experience the reality that as spiritual beings we each share the same universal energy, while expressing this energy in individual configurations of unique energy signatures.

When we watch a movie, we know that it is not real, yet we willingly suspend our disbelief so as to enter into the vicarious experience of the drama being projected onto the screen. If we can do this—and we all do it so easily—we can use this same ability in reverse to exit the drama that ensues from being an ego in a body. We can willingly suspend our belief in it.

Loving Yourself

FEAR COMES WITH the territory of being human and in the body. All of our perceived wrongdoings emanate from the primal fear of separation from our divine Self. Try as we may to drop fear, we still carry it with us. It seems Krazy Glued to our coattails.

It is when we are in the grip of anxiety that we call out to whoever will hear us for a way to escape. "Please," we say, "take this away from me." This is when we have an opportunity to break with the habit of seeking relief and succor from an outside source.

At such a time, we can call upon our true Self to speak to our egoic self and say, "It's okay, all is well." In this way, we weaken the grip of fear emanating from the false self and reinforce the reality of our true Self.

No matter how much we talk about our oneness with God, *experiencing* our oneness is the only way we truly come to remember this oneness. *A Course in Miracles* states, "A universal theology is impossible, but a universal *experience* is not only possible but necessary." [14]

How can you be the love of God in a situation? Ask yourself how God would act. Then do just that. What would God say in this situation? Say just that!

When I visit my medical practitioner, often she shares personal anecdotes with me. On one such occasion, she explained how she came to like having to get up in the middle of the night to deliver babies. She told me of the time when the phone rang in the middle of the night and she made the shift to saying to herself, "This is God calling." This was a shift to correct perception, since indeed we are all the one divine Self. She got up from bed and headed to the phone, then to the hospital with cheerful alacrity.

Now, how would you respond to a caller if you *truly* believed you were responding to God? How would you listen if you knew it was God talking? Imagine the positive effect you would have on others if you became alert Presence listening to them. Imagine if you listened to them with the attention you would give them if you saw them as the divine Self they truly are. Who would not give to the empty hand, if they knew it was God asking? Who would not smile in gratitude if they knew that it was God serving their meal?

CHAPTER EIGHT

Noble Intention

*I*N 1996, I SHARED WITH ONE OF my business colleagues that I wanted to deepen my spirituality. It so happened that he had just met a man who had arrived from England a few weeks earlier, who was said to be a spiritual teacher. "I'll ask if he would be open to leading sessions in your office," he said.

A week later, at the end of the workday, our office door opened and in walked a gentle, unassuming man who was introduced to me as Eckhart Tolle. Almost immediately, I recognized what a profound and timely teacher he was, especially for the West. Each week, Eckhart led us deeper into stillness and spiritual awareness.

As time passed, I learned that Eckhart was writing a book, and in due course he asked me to be his publisher. I had never published a book before, but I felt compelled to make *The Power of Now* available to the world. We joined in oneness, setting our intention, without any sense of whether a handful of people or millions would read it. The book came out in 1998, defying publishing norms as it spread by word of mouth, without advertising. Today it has sold almost four million copies and is available in over 30 languages. It was the child of joining in oneness with a spiritual intent.

Intention is conscious creation through focused thought energized by feeling.

Intention is causative. To intend is requisite to creating. It precedes visualization. Often people feel that if they visualize something, they are creating it. But visualization is only a tool, not the creative source. The same is true of prayer, whether it is uttered verbally or silently. Indeed, both visualization and prayer are fostered by and flow from intent.

Intent is more formless than visualization and prayer, and therefore carries a more refined and powerful creative energy.

Intent is an expression of faith. It is something that is strongly held but not controlled by will, mental effort, or manipulation. Although intent holds to an end state, this end state is not specific in detail and has its own characteristic feeling-signature.

Take the example of holding to the intent of having a healthy relationship. You make no assumptions as to *how* the healthy relationship will be achieved. Intent does not prescribe what is necessary for your relationship to be healthy. As you hold to your intent, the relationship just naturally becomes healthier, in the most appropriate ways. You may be quite surprised by what follows. For example, you may find yourself speaking more openly, honestly, and spontaneously to your partner, without having planned to do so. You may find yourself with a new awareness of your partner's challenges, which leads to a deeper understanding and level of caring in your relationship. You may find more time for each other. And even if you don't, the time you spend together, although perhaps even more limited, may result in your becoming more deeply devoted to each other.

When you hold to an intent, it does not mean that you are passive. On the contrary, holding to your intent requires an investment of energy. This energy may feel strange to you at first. Although there is a thought component to intent, it is not mental energy that is required but heart energy. Whatever needs to be done through or by you will become evident. The guidance you require will often be given at the precise moment you need it. When the spiritual power of the universe is unleashed, watch what happens! This is when we experience synchronicities, delightful "accidents," coincidences, and what we call miracles. There is no grand announcement or fanfare, just amazing results.

While all intention is powerful, intention can arise from two different sources. The effect in each case is also quite different.

Intention can be ego-based. This often involves a desire for status, prestige, power, and wealth. Your intentions are wrapped up with yourself, so they tend to be narcissistic. It's all about you—your comfort, security, and success.

Ego-based intention, no matter how positive it may appear, is actually rooted in the negative emotion of fear. Driven by a sense of personal lack, it is need-based. When intention springs from your feelings of inadequacy, you have a need to prove something to yourself and perhaps others.

When intention is based in ego, you may accomplish a great deal. The more you feel you have to prove, the more likely you are to hone your intentions in a powerful way. But intention that is ego-based bears the hallmark of a voracious vacuum sucking into itself. Whenever intention emanates from an egoic state of mind, the good it can achieve is restricted by the boundaries of self-interest.

Intention can also be what I call "noble." Whether or not an intent is noble is determined by the motivation behind it. If an intent is noble, it will not be based on egoic need and gratification.

Instead of being motivated primarily by money, fame, or power, noble intention is love-based and flows from your heart. You come from a higher consciousness, and your intentions are simply an expression of the goodness within you. It is a noble intention primarily because it concerns your own spiritual growth or the betterment of others. Your focus is on the possibilities for blessing the world, not on personal gain.

When you hold to a noble intention, you are coming from the core of your being, which is love. Your intention, the initial stage of creativity, is an extension of your true Self. Because its accomplishments are the fruit of love, they bring about lasting good for you and for all concerned.

After stressing the importance of noble intent, Jesus added that everything you require will be given to you, "pressed down, shaken together, and running over."[15] When you seek only the noble, your divine Self will withhold nothing. This is because it is safe to shower you with all good things, since you will not use these things in service of the ego. Because your motivation is not money, you will not be attached to financial abundance when it comes to you. You can fully and joyfully appreciate it in the present moment, but you will not fear losing it. *You* then own your money—*it* doesn't own you. Although abundance is not the motivation of your intent, it comes back to you in all forms as the byproduct of it.

Prestige may come with your success. But because it wasn't sought after, you will remain free of ego and not be attached to your higher profile. You will enjoy the higher personal profile, not as a matter of self-importance, but because of the doors it opens to you for further avenues of service. You will have no egoic need to hold on to it.

When you take the power of intention and make it noble by using it for the good of another, or humanity in general, you ignite it with spiritual rocket fuel. Being causative, such an intention can only bring about positive results. Because it is without ego, expect quicker manifestation, since ego impedes progress with fear-based worry, doubt, hesitation, and vacillation.

Since what you are doing is not in service of the ego, the result cannot be anything but a blessing to others. And when others are blessed, the one who holds the intention is also blessed. It is a spiritual law that when we love, we are loved. And when we bless, we are blessed.

It is up to each of us to invest our actions with a higher purpose. For example, you can produce a movie in order to become famous or wealthy, or you can do the same from noble intent, seeking only to elevate the consciousness of viewers. Both require intent, but one is ego-based and the other noble.

Live Intentionally Every Day

THE RICHES OF NOBLE INTENT are always available for harvesting, no matter what your particular walk of life.

Suppose you work in a bakery. Are you merely making cakes? Or are you making delights that will enhance the celebration when folk get together?

Someone may say, "But I work in a mailroom. With little formal education, this is likely where I will work for the rest of my life. What possibility is there for me to invest my work with noble intention, and to do something significant for others?"

If you work in a mailroom, you may wish to expand your service territory. Hold to the intent to be of greater use in some way that fulfills you. Plant the mustard seed of noble intent and see what happens.

In the meantime, hold to the intent to continue in gainful employment in order to support your family—a noble activity. If you have no family to support, hold to the intent to continue to be self-supporting—again, a noble thing.

There is something else you can do. You can intend to be a radiating center of love in your workplace, bringing a smile and warm acceptance to all you encounter.

On a trip from Vancouver, BC, to Los Angeles, I had to pass through U.S. customs. It wasn't busy that morning, so no one was marshalling us into particular lines. Since I could choose whichever customs officer I wanted to go to, I scanned their faces, and one caught my eye. His expression was warm, his countenance inviting.

"You marked the purpose of your trip as both personal and business," he said.

"Yes, I'm speaking at a church in Orange County," I explained. "I am a publisher, and the congregation has read a number of the books I have published. Given the success story of my small publishing house and our publishing mission, they wanted to hear what I had to say."

"What areas do you publish in?" the officer asked.

"Spirituality and self-help," I said.

"Spirituality!" he exclaimed. "That's what we need. You know, I am not really a customs officer. I am an undercover blesser. Working as a customs officer is a way to meet people. If I didn't meet you, how could I bless you?" He nodded at a group of people who entered at that moment. "Look at all these people. Look at how many I get to bless."

"You don't need my talk!" I responded. "But I sure am going to tell my audience about you."

"Have a wonderful trip," he said with a smile.

This was a United States customs officer! Instead of feeling under suspicion or intimidated, I was received with a welcome and warmth.

This officer left me with an awareness of the goodness to be found in the most unexpected places and people.

Conscious people can't help but give of their divine attributes. Everything they do is intentional. How different this is from what most of us do as we pursue our daily routines. We are often upset, moody, critical, complaining. It's as though we save our blessing of people for Sunday. "Peace be with you," we chorus, never thinking of blessing people in this way all week long. But here was a man who allowed his divine Self to flow into his everyday life, every day.

In Hebrew literature we encounter a man named Jabez, who asked Yahweh, "Oh, that You would bless me indeed, and enlarge my territory, that Your hand would be with me, and that You would keep me from evil, that I may not cause pain."[16] What a beautiful prayer of noble intention. Jabez sought an expanded, fuller life through being able to be of greater service to others. The "territory" he was asking to be expanded was his service territory. He was like the United States customs officer in that the more people he had to bless, the happier he would be. Jabez considered being able to be of service to others a great blessing. The other thing he asked for was to be able to be of service in a way that was not tainted by ego: "… that You would keep me from evil, that I may not cause pain!"

Jabez teaches us what noble intention is. If you too want to expand your service territory, saying this prayer daily would be a wonderful way to begin doing just that.

Oneness Through Diversity, Not Sameness

WE ARE TOLD that in creating the physical universe, God held an intent, then spoke it into being: "*Let* there be light."[17] When God surveyed what had been created, it was all "good." Being one with God, we are co-creators with God, so our process of creating is the same. Intention is the way we as God's offspring are meant to create.

A Course In Miracles reminds us that in creating, we share in God's creative power. But while God created us, we did not create God. To illustrate the difference, *The Course* explains, "Parents give birth to children, but children do not give birth to parents. They do, however, give birth to their children, and thus give birth as their parents do."[18] This is necessarily so because, if God created us and we created God, there would be a closed circle without possibility of expansion. It would be as if the divine had turned back on itself, allowing itself to be enclosed.

It is important to be clear that "God's accomplishments are not yours." On the other hand, your accomplishments are like God's, because "we are co-creators with God." We are meant to create as God, adding to the diversity of divine self-expression. "Your creations belong in you, as you belong in God. You are part of God, as your sons are part of His Sons."[19]

Many of us have mistaken our oneness with God for sameness. We are not the same—we are diverse. We are unique aspects of the diversity of God. Though the whole of God's *nature* dwells in each of us, there is diversity of creative self-expression in God. In other words, our creative power participates in the divine creativity, but it does so as an *aspect* of the creativity of the divine, and not as the whole of divine creativity.

The divine Self is infinitely diverse, and you and I are its expressions. We will always carry with us the uniqueness of who we are. We will grow and change, but we will each always be a unique aspect of the One.

⌒ Creative Intention

*T*HERE IS A DIFFERENCE between setting a goal and setting an intention. Goals originate in the human mind, are quite defined, and are accomplished by mental willpower and physical effort. Therefore they have limited possibilities. Intent is equally focused, yet it is open to all possibilities.

With a goal, you imagine in your mind's eye the desired outcome and work assiduously step-by-step to achieve it. With intent, you abandon any "efforting" to make specific things happen. You don't need to know how things are going to work out, you just need to trust that they will. Intention utilizes a more refined and powerful creative vibration than setting a goal and carrying it out. Intent requires that you set your intention, then hold to it, hold to it, hold to it—with all your heart.

How do you establish a noble intention?

You cannot manufacture a noble intention, cannot just "think one up." You cannot pluck one out of the air, either. You don't look for a good cause and decide to get involved because it would be a good thing to do. Willing an intention into being is just another form of the mind trying to be in control.

A noble intention has to come from the heart—*your* heart. Hence, noble intentions are highly personal. They are born at the core of your being, the place where your everyday experience of your divine Self interfaces with universal consciousness.

Ask yourself, "How can I bring myself the greatest joy and fulfillment?" If you ask sincerely, you will receive an answer. This is guaranteed. How could it be otherwise, since you are asking your own divine Self, which would never deny you any good thing. Everything we could possibly ask for is waiting for us in potential, awaiting only our sincere asking. As such we can say, "Thank you, my divine Self, for having answered before I have even asked."

You can recognize a noble intention because it comes out of the purity of inner stillness and is not weighed down by thought forms. Noble intentions are made known to us when we listen to that still small voice within us. The key is to be able to *hear* this inner voice of spirit. You can recognize this voice because it comes from a deeper place than the voices you usually hear in your head, and it carries the energy of your heart. This requires discernment.

To discern is quite different from trying to figure things out. It is a "knowing." The hallmark of this "knowing" is that it is devoid of ego. You will know you are receiving your answer when, instead of responding by imagining yourself successful, powerful, or wealthy, it has the confirming sense of a purpose that makes you your most loving, most joyful, most fulfilled self.

During the stage of creation through intent, all the action takes place on the inner dimension. The intention needs to be sustained. It is in sustaining it that you add the fuel that provides the power for its manifestation. Sometimes your intent is in the foreground, sometimes in the background, but it is always there until it produces the manifestation.

Setting a noble intention is not a one-time act. Ego can creep into even a noble intention if the intent is not sustained repeatedly. Especially where structure is involved, it is easy for something noble to become egoic. For instance, a person shared with me that he had the opportunity to visit the United Nations in New York City and read the original charter. He read slowly, word by precious word. Then he wept. Why? Because there was such a gap between the original goals of the United Nations and the limited role it is currently playing in our world.

The United Nations is just one of several institutions that were founded on noble intentions, but that have strayed from these. Government, churches, free enterprise, medicine, education—all started out with laudable goals, being principle-based and many of them also heart-centered. But over time, as structures developed to support them, they moved to being mind-centered and veered from their initial vision and purpose. They moved away from a belief in the goodness of people, thinking that they needed more control over people to protect them from themselves. They began fostering separation and dependence. Henry David Thoreau said it well: "That government is best which governs least." This goes for all institutions. Why? Because the more form or structure you have, the more ego you will find there. Structure by its nature separates instead of unites. It leads to a distancing of those who serve from the very ones who were meant to be served. In addition, the maintenance of the structure itself requires time and energy, thereby taking away from the focus of the original purpose of the organization.

When you have a noble intention that runs throughout your life, it is likely part of your soul mission for this incarnation. In such a case, the noble intention remains constant, while the form of its expression usually changes over your lifetime.

In my own experience, throughout my work life I have wanted people to recognize their magnificence as offspring of God. This intent was held through my careers of English teacher, management consultant, publisher, and now author. Different roles, same intent. As I look back, I see the thin golden thread that connected all of these professions, enabling me to bring forward skills learned from one career into the next.

As you sustain your noble intention, life presents you with more challenging and expansive ways to be of service. Your sphere of influence will likely also continue to increase, reaching larger and larger communities as the intention is sustained.

How the law of intent works is depicted in the so-called miracle stories of Jesus. You see it in the changing of water into wine at a wedding feast in Cana, which resulted in an over-abundance of the finest wine. This superfluity is also the point of the story of the disciples casting their net and drawing in a huge catch of fish, after having fished in vain all night. There were so many fish, the net was in danger of breaking. And, too, the incident of the feeding of a crowd of thousands, when Jesus multiplied five loaves and three little fish, teaches the same lesson of abundance. Once the crowd had eaten their fill, baskets of bread were still left over. These images, not meant to be literalized, reveal that when we invoke loving action with our noble intent, our divine Self will always supply in abundance.

The Power of Joining in Noble Intention

EVERYWHERE WE LOOK, life teaches us the powerful outcome of joining—man to woman, atoms to molecules, seed with soil, sperm with egg. It is in joining that our bodies and all forms of life beyond the single cell amoeba are created. This is so obvious that often we don't stop to marvel at the wonder of creation.

There are other forms of joining that, although less dramatic or visible to the eye, are just as miraculous. When Jesus tried to explain what the kingdom of God is like, he compared it to a mustard seed that a man took and threw into his garden, where it grew and became a tree, and the birds of the air sheltered in its branches. He also compared it to the yeast a woman took and mixed in with three measures of flour until it was leavened throughout. Mustard seed and yeast could not create the kingdom on their own. They required joining—the seed with soil, the yeast with flour.

Joining with another or others in noble intent is a sacred act. It is a partnership of spirits who join without selfish motive, hidden agendas, or wobbly commitment.

Jesus, a master of intent, spoke of this power of joining in noble intent when he said, "Where two or more are gathered in *My name*, there I am also."[20] The expression "My name" refers to the consciousness of Jesus—his divine nature. When two or more join in loving intent, out of the conjoined heart energy comes greater creativity. The creative power of love, present in each person who aligns with the same intent, supports and propels it into manifestation. When there is true joining of hearts, the power to quickly manifest a right outcome multiplies according to the numbers involved in the sacred joining and the strength of the energy charge behind their intent.

This is the kind of power that can quickly change our reality. When atoms join to form molecules, a powerful energy is emitted. Similarly, when we join with others in noble intent, we let loose a powerful redemptive force into our world.

Suppose you are an architect joining with city planners, a priest joining with a congregation, or a doctor joining with a patient. How can you know whether you are joining nobly?

When egos join, they usually do so because they want something *from* the other, not *for* the other. Since noble intention does not come from ego, there is no selfishness in the parties who join together in it. Neither is the intent you hold dependent on another holding it with you. A test of whether your intent is noble is if the other withdrew their intent, would you still sustain yours?

When we come from noble intent, we don't join with others out of personal need but because we hold the same heart energy around an intent. The parties also intuitively know that in their joining, they greatly increase the power of their intent to manifest quickly.

Since noble intention emanates from our inner Presence, when we join with another, we are joining them in the oneness of Presence. This is perhaps the quickest and most confirming way to experience our Oneness.

Some of us have had the good fortune to sit with others in a group meditation or spiritual teaching and experience the profound power of collective Presence. To be able to facilitate such an experience of Presence is one of the gifts of the spiritual master. Being so completely one with their own inner Presence, the spiritual master acts like a bonfire, drawing the smaller flames of Presence into one mighty blaze.

This is what happened on the Day of Pentecost, after Jesus' departure from his disciples. He had been their spiritual master, preparing them for a task. On this particular day, a hundred and twenty people had gathered together "with one accord."[21] The flame that flickered in each of them suddenly ignited into a blaze of Presence. Their mission in the world could now begin.

This powerful aura of Presence has been referred to in the East as our "Buddha field." But we don't need to wait to sit with a master in order to benefit from this field. We need only recognize and cultivate our own inner Presence and *be* this Presence in the world.

Opportunities to experience oneness in joint intention are everywhere. They are often found with what on the surface may seem like the most unlikely partners.

One day when visiting my daughter, I forgot to make sure our dog Bijoux came into the apartment building after me. It was about half an hour later that I realized he wasn't with us. Panic struck. Thoughts of him being lost and getting hit by a car or picked up by someone who might abuse him consumed me. In this state of high anxiety, I ran out to search for him. Up and down streets and alleyways I raced, into neighborhood stores and restaurants, asking anyone I met if they had seen a small bichon frise on the loose. Most were so busy in their own worlds, they showed little concern. Then, down one alley, I stumbled upon two homeless dumpster divers. They immediately sensed my state of high anxiety, and before I could speak asked me what was wrong. They listened with their full attention, expressed sincere concern, joined me in intent to find Bijoux, then came up with a strategy to search for him, each taking a different area to scour. Yes, Bijoux was found safe and sound, but that incident affected me profoundly. In our joining in intent, I felt so close, so in love with those two dumpster divers. It was a sacred experience of oneness. I am now forever joined at the heart level with these two precious beings, although predictably I will never meet them again. Because of that incident, I now bless each homeless person with increased intensity.

There are no boundaries and no impediments to joining in intent. Gender, nationality, religion, or geographical distance do not enter the picture. In intent, we can experience the reality of our oneness with anyone, anywhere in the world. Through such joining, we tap into the Power of One.

CHAPTER NINE

The Evolutionary Path to the Leap

*E*VEN THOUGH OUR NATURE is an expression of divinity, most of us do not see much that is divine about the way humans have conducted themselves on this planet to date. Why is this?

To make sense of the presently limited expression of divine characteristics such as love, joy, and peace in our species, we need an understanding of how the divine becomes expressed in the material realm.

In some religious traditions, the central belief is that we are individual souls, created by a God who is wholly other than us. These traditions emphasize our separateness from God and our need to honor our Creator.

In other traditions, the dominant view is that our physical existence is an illusion, not real. It is as if God was having a dream, and we are all characters in the dream. Once again, the basic idea is our separation from the divine, albeit a separation that is illusory.

In both these views, the focus is on healing the separation between ourselves and the divine by becoming free of the material realm and returning to the divine.

Instead of seeing God as separate from the physical realm, the Leap recognizes that the whole of material existence is also God. It is God incarnate, the body of God. It is all divine "stuff"—God's own being, not something separate from God. Creation is an act of divine self-expression, not the making of something that is outside of God. In other words, nothing but God exists.

God is the consciousness in all things. This consciousness seeks to emerge fully in the material realm through us. But its emergence in us, like the emergence of the elementary particles that make up matter, and then the more evolved forms of matter, is an evolutionary process.

Human evolution involves God becoming fully conscious of itself in form through us. The Leap involves humans moving into God consciousness. We are not casting aside our human form, but using it as a means to become fully conscious.

Almost a thousand years ago, a Sufi teacher expressed this so clearly and succinctly:

> God sleeps in the rock,
> Dreams in the plant,
> Stirs in the animal, and
> Awakens in humankind.[22]

⁓ The Evolution of
Consciousness into Matter

CONSCIOUSNESS IS ALL-EMBRACING—a universal one-ness of all that is material and immaterial, actual and potential. But when consciousness incarnates, it can only express itself to the degree that the form it incarnates into is sufficiently evolved in complexity to recognize then express it.

A quick overview of evolution shows that consciousness has manifested itself as increasingly complex in form—atoms, molecules, plants, flowers, reptiles, mammals. The greater the degree of complexity, the greater the potential is for the expression of consciousness.

As the offspring of God, our incarnation as pure consciousness in bodily form is a process spanning eons of time. In the stage we have been in for a long time now, it fools us into believing we are the animal costume we wear.

Consciousness evolved an animal body, then the body took it to be just that—a body, not consciousness *in the form of a body.* It was at this moment, as we evolved self-reflective consciousness, that the ego was born.

With body identification came many of the ills we are still grappling with, all born of fear—projection, blame, judgment, defensiveness, aggression, abuse, self-centeredness, hoarding.

Consider how prevalent fear is in our lives. Fear of failure, fear of success, fear of poverty, fear of abundance (yes, this too). Fear of an employer, fear of a spouse, fear of a neighbor, fear of other nations. Fear of illness, fear of pain, fear of death. In our misidentification of ourselves as merely a body, we ensure that fear infiltrates every dimension of life.

In the early stages of our human evolution, when our capacity for connection was limited and we lived in the delusion that we were all alone, we feared those who seemed to be "others." *Us* and *them* became our dominant mentality, and with this the need to defend ourselves against *them*. Fear drove much of what we have come to label as animalistic behavior, such as obsequious homage to the leader who has the most might, the setting up of territorial boundaries, protection of kin and clan at all cost, and preying off those who are weaker. We even feared our own essence—our divine Self—and created religions based on this fear.

Because we are not inherently separate, only deluded into believing we are, we cannot help being drawn into groups. Consequently, humans have increasingly been driven to unite in larger and larger groups—extended families, clans, tribes, nations, and empires. But these alliances have always proved fragile because they are based on belief in *us* and *them*. Only as we become increasingly conscious of our oneness can we truly end our separateness.

We have reached the time in our long evolutionary journey where we are capable of recognizing our connection to everyone and everything. As a result, we are now ready to leave our sense of separation behind and move into consciousness of our oneness. When a sufficient number of us—the requisite critical mass—have attained unity consciousness, the rest of our species will be drawn into it. Then, fear of each other and fear of God will go out the window.

In simplest terms, this is what the Leap is about—leaving the limitations of the ego behind and evolving into being able to express our divine oneness in incarnate form. The ego separates—it cannot see unity. The divine joins—it sees only one Self.

So much of daily life as we currently experience it is determined by our feelings of separation and the fear that accompanies this. The personal and global outcome of transcending all sense of separation, thereby ending all fear, is peace. Peace of mind, peace in families, peace among communities and the world's nations. I think we all sense that this must be the next step for our species—a leap we can no longer avoid if we are to survive.

Reaching Critical Mass

WHEN THE DIVINE MANIFESTS in material form, it requires a long evolutionary process in which there are no shortcuts. In the way most people think of "miracles," there are no miracles that quicken the incarnation process. Pure consciousness cannot instantly materialize in full-blown human form. To date, science tells us that the journey into human form has taken something like 13 billion years. Only now are we at the point where we are able to come fully into divine consciousness as a species.

It has only been within the last 3,000 years that we have seen the beginning of realizing our divine consciousness through rare individuals who were harbingers of what is to become, hopefully in our time, a reality for the whole world. We have already seen that there is growing evidence of this happening, as more and more individuals come into consciousness of our oneness. Today, the nucleus of the critical mass is forming.

Viewing evolutionary history, it is clear that it has been punctuated by leaps that have accelerated the journey into form. But these are not the result of interventions by some external hand, in the way that people often picture God intervening to perform miracles. Rather, these leaps occur when critical mass is attained, pushing a species across a threshold. The new form that has been developing then breaks through as the dominant form.

As an example, we see how mammals rapidly populated the world once the reign of the dinosaurs ended. They had been evolving, and leapt to prominence once reptiles were largely exterminated, which geology tells us was most likely the result of a meteorite with the mass of Mount Everest slamming into what is today the Yucatan peninsula.[23]

While no external God intervenes to hurry the process along with "miracles," the *entire* process is miraculous. It is the work of consciousness "outpressing" itself into form that builds in complexity. Evolution needs no external God to intervene and move it forward, no external God to guide it, because evolution itself is divine. Evolution is miracle. It is the flowering of consciousness in form.

Walt Whitman captures the essence of how God is incarnate in the very fabric of form when he writes:

> I know nothing else but miracles. Whether I walk the streets of Manhattan, or dart my sight over the roofs of houses toward the sky, or wade with naked feet along the beach just in the edge of the water, or stand under trees in the woods, or talk by day with any one I love, or sleep in bed at night with anyone I love, or sit at table at dinner with the rest, or look at strangers opposite me riding in the car, or watch honey-bees busy around the hive of a summer forenoon, or animals feeding in the fields, or birds, or the wonderfulness of insects in the air, or the exquisite delicate thin curve of the new moon in spring. These with the rest, one and all, are to me miracles, the whole referring, yet each distinct and in its place. To me every hour of the light and dark is a miracle, every cubic inch of space is a miracle, every square yard of the surface of the earth is spread with miracles, every foot of the interior swarms with miracles.[24]

Whitman's expression "the whole referring, yet each distinct and in its place" is a reference to the "one in the many"—the oneness of the true Self of all beings manifested in countless diverse forms, each of them an incarnate reflection of pure consciousness.

As consciousness incarnates, it necessarily loses self-awareness. There is no way around this: it has to be. This loss of awareness occurs because, while the whole of the material realm is the manifestation of consciousness, the forms that carry this consciousness are at first simple and not capable of self-awareness. Consciousness is expressed in everything, but only in tiny "packets" (the meaning of the scientific term *quanta*, as in quantum mechanics), which means that its manifestation is fragmentary and limited.

Matter itself is consciousness in diffuse form. But there is a small "packet" of pure consciousness in *everything*, even the most elementary particles. This is the "brain" of all forms—the center that instructs them, much like our autonomic nervous system regulates our bodies without us having to think of the countless systems that function from moment to moment, day to day, year to year.

But while an atom is a coming together of "packets" of consciousness, which is what gives it its order, it is but a rudimentary expression of consciousness. Only when consciousness becomes concentrated in highly developed, complex forms does self-awareness—consciousness of ourselves—become possible.

We might liken this to droplets of water, which when gathered together form the oceans. Though raindrops and oceans are essentially identical in nature, a raindrop is able to manifest the characteristics of water only in limited form. While a single raindrop contains the potential of an ocean, when it lands on your body in a spring shower, it does not feel at all heavy. Accumulate enough raindrops in a large drum, however, and you cannot lift it. Accumulate an ocean of raindrops, and it exhibits forces that, while inherent in the raindrop, are only experienced when raindrops are concentrated.

"God is love," say the Scriptures. Since everything that exists is the self-manifestation of God, love is the underlying reality of the universe.

This is why all material forms, from the simplest particles to complex creatures including ourselves, experience attraction. All attraction, all joining of material forms, is divine love. Whether atoms join as molecules to form elements, or humans unite as couples, all such joining is divine love in expression.

The self-awareness of humans that enables them to form relationships is now beginning to undergo a further intensification, as we recognize that the whole of reality is a single fabric—a oneness. Transcending even self-awareness, this level of consciousness is now essential to the survival of humanity. For at the level of full-blown divine consciousness, we recognize in each other the same one Self that is our own being. This recognition is what will heal our fractured planet, uniting us in form as we have always been united in divine essence.

The recognition of ourselves as expressions of the one Self is the experience of unlimited divine consciousness in material form—an experience lost to us through eons of evolutionary time because of the very nature of the process. A fullness of love, a fullness of joy, and a fullness of peace can only become our everyday experience when the whole of reality becomes aware of all of its parts as the expression of the one Self that is the essence of each of us.

As human beings, we were *meant* to get lost and feel separate from our divine Source. The divine cannot journey into self-manifestation as form by any other means. All of the chaos, confusion, and at times outright nightmarish horror of the human condition are necessary byproducts of the journey. Creatures experiencing only a fragmentary consciousness are simply not capable of the joyous and totally loving experience of oneness that is their essence as pure consciousness, and that is now on the verge of flourishing in human form.

To be lost in a fragmentary state, and to reunite in full oneness in form, has a dynamic energy that propels creation forward. As more of us come into this realization, the consciousness we experience increases exponentially.

∿ *A Parable Portrays Human Evolution*

*J*ESUS TOLD A PARABLE about a prodigal son. The prodigal takes all of his inheritance from his father, leaves home, and dissipates his fortune through profligate living. When he has exhausted his means of support, he remembers his father, and trusts his father will still take him back, if even as a servant.

When the son goes home, his father, anticipating his return, sees him coming at a distance and runs out to greet him with a loving embrace. Then he sends his servant to bring his son sandals, a robe, and a ring before he enters the village. No one is to know the depths of degradation to which the son had sunk. When they see him, he will look just like he did when he departed.

Arriving home, the father calls for the slaughter of the fattest calf. A feast is prepared in his son's honor. Learning of this, his second son— the one who stayed at home—asks his father why he is celebrating the return of his prodigal brother, when he himself has been a faithful son and at his father's side all his life—and yet no celebration was ever thrown in his honor. This son represents the vision and voice of the ego. From the ego's perspective, there does seem to be unfairness here. This is because the ego only ever gives in order to get something. It keeps score.

The son who stayed at home was dutiful, but expects a reward in return for fulfilling his duty. The father sees with the eyes of love and tells his faithful son that his brother was lost, and now is found, and this is cause for celebration.

When we awaken from our long spiritual evolutionary slumber and return "home" to claim our divine heritage, the whole of creation will celebrate.

CHAPTER TEN

Radical Forgiveness

THE LEAP REQUIRES US to let go of all that is not truly who we are as our divine Self. This includes anything that causes us to feel less than adequate, self-critical, or guilty. The human condition by its very nature means that we are plagued with regret, often expressed in the form of a myriad statements about what we "would have," "should have," or "could have" said or done.

Coming into this world with its culture of insanity means that we all take on some of this insanity. Consequently, we don't see clearly or accurately. When we act on misperceptions, we create situations that we come to regret. Then we call these "mistakes."

What wisdom we hold in hindsight! To grow up, we have to make lots of "mistakes." But as adults, we look back and realize that these "mistakes" were essential to our development. Set against a backdrop of our evolution into form, the things we call mistakes also take on a new meaning. They become hidden gifts, to be unwrapped and examined as a means of coming into fuller awareness of our divine Self. Times when we miss the mark and end up experiencing guilt and regret are opportunities to be thankful for, as they alert us to areas of our lives in which we still need to express the loving person we truly are.

A Course In Miracles reminds us, "Whenever you are not wholly joyous, it is because you have reacted with a lack of love to one of God's creations."[25] I add that it is also because we have withheld love from *ourselves*.

Ask your inner knower to show you where in your life you are withholding love. Then, watch what emerges not only from within, as your awareness expands, but also in the circumstances of your outer world. You will see that the situations you find yourself in mirror back to you the precise areas of your life where your love has yet to flourish.

You Are Not a Victim

WHEN WE THINK OF ourselves as victims, we never heal. Because we see things as coming to us from outside of ourselves, we perceive ourselves as having little control over what happens to us. This generates fear, causes us to experience feelings of hopelessness, and incites us to blame someone or something else for our condition.

By giving our power away to external circumstances, we cut ourselves off from the only true means of healing—and the only way to change our experiences—which is found within ourselves. And so we remain victims.

The root of feeling like a victim lies not in what happens to us from outside ourselves, but in the fact that we do not recognize that we love ourselves. Self-love is the great healer, but our conditioning blocks the soothing flow of the love that we are.

To shed your victim mentality involves being with yourself and allowing yourself to feel your own love—no matter what may have happened or is happening to you. It involves feeling the love you are, in all the dimensions of your being, especially those you have tended to disown.

When you start to embrace your whole self and allow yourself to feel the unconditional love that is your very essence, you discover that you are not and never have been separate from the loving Presence that permeates the universe. How could you be, when you are that love?

Once you begin to experience your oneness with everyone and everything, you realize that even in the victimization you perceive yourself as having suffered, you were never anything but loved. All of your experiences that have caused you pain, regret, or guilt were steeped in the loving Presence that is always bringing healing and wholeness.

Ending the feeling that we are victims involves accepting that, as co-creators of our experiences, we are one hundred percent responsible for everything we allow in our lives—everything. If we do not like some of what we experience, we can change it. This is how we heal ourselves and our world, since the world of form is simply an "outpressing" of our inner reality.

It has been said, "The holiest of all the spots on earth is where an ancient hatred has become a present love."[26] When this occurs, it is because we are now seeing accurately. We recognize that the hurt we inflicted on another was nothing more than our inability at the time of the hurt to express the love we really are.

Once again, viewed as a part of our evolution, we realize that the many times we "get it wrong" are how we learn to act with authenticity, responsibility, and integrity. This is how the evolution of consciousness proceeds.

A common misconception, often promoted by religions, is that for-giveness somehow involves the balancing of scales of justice. Such a con-cept assumes the world was originally flawless, and we messed it up. But from an evolutionary standpoint, there never was a time in which the world was flawless. On the contrary, evolution proceeds by trial and error. At the personal and social level, when we hurt badly enough from our choices, we eventually no longer wish to be either hurt or hurtful and begin making better choices.

When asked how often we should forgive, Jesus responded, "Seventy times seven." This is a symbol of infinity. Jesus understood that we come into our own through trial and error, and that sometimes we will need to make poor choices countless times before we discover the advantages of becoming more responsible.

No matter how many times we create painful situations for ourselves and others, there really is nothing to forgive. There are no scales to bal-ance. There is only a person or situation to which we need to extend our love in a fuller way than we have been capable of until now. Forgiveness is the act of releasing our dammed-up love and letting it flow. It becomes available *for giving*.

Still, there is an aspect of forgiveness that invites us to turn to our brother or sister and express our desire for their forgiveness. There is noth-ing negative in this. We are saying, "I would like another opportunity to show you what a loving person I truly am, because I have not shown you this about myself." So we pick up the telephone, or we buy the bouquet of flowers that has "Sorry" written all over it—and if necessary, we make reparations. This is not "undoing" some supposed evil, but simply mov-ing forward in manifesting the love that is our true nature.

Having said this, you can forgive but not necessarily reestablish a rela-tionship. A woman chose to part from her two aunts earlier in her life because they came from such judgment and negativity. Years later she received a surprising card in the mail asking for forgiveness from one of them. In truth, she could not remember the specifics of what the aunts had said and done to cause her to move away from their energy. She replied with a card, stating that she could remember nothing that needed to be forgiven, but was happy to extend her forgiveness if the aunt felt she needed to hear it.

It was clear that the aunt wanted to restore their relationship. But the niece knew that it was not appropriate for her to go back into that relationship. Her inner knower told her that to extend an invite to meet with her aunts now would have been inauthentic and therefore not in spiritual integrity. Forgiveness is given and received on a higher level than human drama. Whether two people consider restoring a relationship is then a matter of choice, guided by the inner knower.

Whether a relationship is restored or not, what a gift forgiveness brings to our brothers and sisters, as each of us is blessed with a sense of promoting each other's wellbeing along this evolutionary journey. To refuse to give forgiveness to others prevents us from being able to give it to ourselves. We are here to forgive each other until we no longer need each other for this purpose.

Why Forgiving Yourself Is Difficult

THE MAJORITY OF US find it easier to forgive others than to forgive ourselves. This is because self-judgment is deeply embedded in our unconscious from infancy, and likely from past lifetimes. What is the source of such self-judgment?

Michael Brown points out in *The Presence Process* that we are unconditional love born into a conditional world that withholds unconditional love from us. This causes us to believe we are broken, not good enough, unworthy, even bad. If we weren't, we tell ourselves, we would experience only unconditional love.

Seeking unconditional love from others is like looking for a breath of fresh air in the depths of the ocean, says Michael. He adds that "if we want to experience a breath of fresh air in the depths of the ocean, we had better make sure we place it down there ourselves."[27] How do we find unconditional love in a conditional world? We have to put it there ourselves—and keep putting it there, and putting it there, until it prevails.

We find it hard to forgive ourselves because to do so means we will have to drop the kind of thinking that the mind tells us will protect us, when it actually makes us vulnerable to the negative energy of self-judgment. Our conditioned mind says, "You need to be a good boy, a good girl. You need to be perfect in order to be lovable and loved. If you are good, you will be safe." Of course, as soon as we are not perfect, we feel unsafe. Fear takes over. We may be afraid of punishment, or just simply afraid for no particular reason. As long as the egoic mind holds us in the grip of fear, we cannot love ourselves unconditionally. We fail to see that love is our nature.

Self-criticism perpetuates the strength of the self-punishing ego because it keeps us in a state of fear. The greatest fear we have is of receiving a whipping from our egoic self. This becomes obvious when we repeat our addictive behavior and continue to beat ourselves up after each "lapse." Since the worse we feel about ourselves, the more likely we are to repeat the addictive behavior to make ourselves feel better, beating ourselves up ensures the addiction continues!

All self-judgment is irrational. Just listen to your self-talk around self-judgment and see how absolutely crazy it is. It's from our irrational self-judgment and accompanying lack of self-forgiveness that we create much of our inner drama. Self-talk, in all forms, feeds drama. When our self-talk stops, we not only forgive ourselves, but our drama falls away, making room for inner peace. Of course, the ego will fight to prevent this, since it is sustained by drama! Now we can see why it is some-time easier to forgive others than to forgive ourselves. When we look at others, we don't hear the nonsensical mental chatter going on in their head, so it is easier to forgive them.

⌁ The Perfection of Imperfection

A S WE HAVE SEEN, victims can never heal because they see things as coming to them from outside of themselves, so they are in a constant state of fear, hopelessness, and blame. They have given their power away to other people or to external situations, while the only true power to heal and change our experiences is to be found within ourselves.

An aspect of the Leap we need to take is to cease being dependent on others for assurance that we are forgiven. When we no longer look to others for validation, but to our own inherent divinity, we simply forgive ourselves.

But *how* are we to forgive ourselves?

The word "forgive" literally means "for giving." Associated with giving are words such as affectionate, altruistic, amicable, benevolent, charitable, compassionate, comprehending, generous, humane, kindly, tender. Do you hear any overtones of groveling or self-recrimination in these words? On the contrary, they invite gentleness with ourselves, being easy on ourselves, being understanding of ourselves.

Forgiveness comes when we quiet our punishing self-talk by entering into stillness. Becoming still, we automatically create a space in which the unconditional love we long to experience can surface from beneath our self-criticism. The love is there—it always has been—and will arise spontaneously whenever we enter into stillness.

The next time you hear the voice of your ego in your head criticizing you for something—and you *will* hear it, because this voice is loud and insistent—simply become still. By entering into stillness, you foster awareness of the love that is your true nature.

How beautiful it is to see another with all their seeming flaws and love them not only in spite of these flaws, but *because* of them. When we start loving others with all of their seeming faults, we can then forgive ourselves for these same faults. Put another way, when we can see our own frailty in others and can forgive them, then we can forgive ourselves for the same frailty.

In loving others in their unconsciousness, we are then able to forgive our own unconsciousness. To see the thief and love him in his thievery, see the addict and love her in her addiction, is to encourage transformation in both the other and ourselves. To see in the seeming weakness of another the beauty of their struggle is to see through the illusion to the reality of love behind and within all things.

There is then a sense in which there is perfection in imperfection. Divine love cannot be fully expressed until humanity has reached a stage in our evolutionary journey at which enough consciousness is present. Yet, each stage of the journey, though in one sense incomplete, manifests a perfection of its own. Our journey is perfect in that each stage is necessary for the increase of consciousness that evolution makes possible.

You and I are, quite simply, miracles. The entire journey from the Big Bang until now, when we are poised to take a global leap into consciousness of our oneness, is a miracle. Every step forward is a miracle. May we come to the same place as Walt Whitman, when he said that he knew nothing else but miracles. When this reality fills our awareness, we cannot help but overflow with gratitude—and gratitude banishes all self-punishment. We simply bask in the process of becoming divine consciousness incarnate in form.

Part I—Conclusion

*T*HROUGH EVOLUTIONARY EYES, the Leap can be seen to draw much of its substance from a prayer that has likely been repeated more than any other prayer in modern history, The Lord's Prayer. Yet, it seems it is only now that we are at a stage in our evolution in consciousness that we are ready to glean its full meaning. Only now can we pray this prayer with the same consciousness that was within Jesus the Christ.

"Our Father."

"I and the Father are one," said Jesus. As a consequence of realizing his oneness with God, Jesus could say, "Everything the Father has is mine." This means that whenever Jesus needed anything, it was spontaneously available to him out of God's infinite supply.

Jesus prayed that we might see that we are one with God in the identical way he was—that we might recognize we are God's self-expression. In other words, God, as our Father, has extended all of the divine attributes to us that Jesus experienced.

What are the attributes of God? Love, joy, peace, harmony—all that is good, positive, healing, wholesome. Because we share in God's attributes, *it is our nature* to experience these qualities. They are our birthright, waiting to be expressed, not something we have to *try* to be.

God also has other attributes, such as omniscience, omnipotence, and omnipresence. You and I share in these too.

Omniscience means that we are capable of knowing what to do when a decision is before us, without having to sweat it. The answer simply arises from inner consciousness, even as Jesus was guided by the Father within him and needed nobody's advice. When we *need* to know, we can know.

Omnipresence means that we are connected to all people in all times and places. We are not isolated individuals who are alone in the universe, but one with the entire created order. So when you enter a room of people you have never met before, you are not meeting strangers. Recognizing this, you can bypass all of the usual struggle to connect. Connection comes easily because you approach people from the position of knowing that in your oneness, you belong together.

Omnipotence means that there is nothing we cannot accomplish that we need to accomplish—indeed, "all power in heaven and on earth" backs up our efforts.[28]

"Who art in heaven."

Heaven isn't a location. Heaven is an inner state. It is living from the truth of our divine Self.

"Hallowed be Thy name."

What is God's name? From time immemorial, God has been recognized as the "I Am." To hallow God's name is to honor the "I Am" that is your very being. It is to live a life that embraces your sacredness.

"Thy kingdom come."

This is not a vague hope for the future. It invites us to align ourselves with what is in fact happening at *every* moment, and will hopefully soon become a global reality as more and more of us enter into awareness of our divine Self and begin living from this new self-understanding.

"Thy will be done."

In this statement, we are assenting to the fact that nothing but God exists, and therefore everything that is happening in our lives is intimately intertwined with the being of God. These words invite us to look through the veil of illusion and see the reality of God in all things. Becoming aware that everything is divine changes how we respond to the events that happen in our lives. Instead of fighting and resisting them, we align ourselves with them, accepting and embracing them.

"On earth as it is in heaven."

There is no separation between earth and heaven. Heaven refers to our inner being, earth to its outer expression. If we are going to experience our divine Self, we will experience it here on earth. If not here on earth, then where?

Spirituality isn't a journey away from matter, it is the embracing of matter as God's self-expression. All of life becomes holy—every moment of every day, and each activity in which we engage.

"Give us this day our daily bread."

This is not a petition but a statement of fact. Everything that we need comes to us from our divine Self, as we need it! The bread given is *daily* bread. This means that we are no longer tortured by time, fretting about how our needs will be met. We can relax and give our full attention to what is on our plate at *this* moment. Then, by using our creative intention, we bring into expression exactly what is required *at the time* it is required.

"And forgive us our debts, as we forgive our debtors."

We are to expect forgiveness. Our own forgiveness is tied to that of others. Just as it is imperative that our divine Self forgives us for the messy process involved in coming into self-expression, so it is imperative that we also forgive others as they too take this journey of incarnating in material form.

Forgiveness flows easily because, in the final analysis, there is ultimately nothing to forgive. There is just God, taking on material form, a sometimes messy process—just like Michelangelo must have made quite a mess when he carved off countless chips of marble to reveal David.

We forgive by seeing through the veil of illusion of separation from God, recognizing that, in our true nature, all of us are flawless expressions of God. Since we are all one with the divine, how can we not see others as inherently flawless? How can we not see ourselves this way?

No matter how much pain we cause each other in the process of remembering our forgotten divine Self, we are all ultimately faultless.

There can be no blame, for we are in this venture together. Realizing this, it becomes easy to be merciful, compassionate, and kind to each other throughout this unfolding process.

"And lead us not into temptation, but deliver us from evil."

Temptation in this prayer has nothing to do with enticement to irresponsible behavior. It has nothing to do with God testing our faithfulness. It has everything to do with learning to live free of our false egoic self, which gets us into all sorts of conundrums.

We are asking for deliverance "from *the* evil," not just evil in general. What is it that is opposed to our true being? It is the false "self"—the ego—which Jesus said must die if our true Self is ever to come into expression.

In light of the Leap, we can see that this prayer invokes our divine Self. It is saying, "Be who you really are. Don't compromise yourself. Then you won't have to learn the hard way that the only real fulfillment in life comes from being true to your divine Self."

PART II

LEAP PRACTICES

*P*ART I OF THIS BOOK stressed the importance of needing to adopt correct perceptions, new behaviors, and new practices in order to break out of humanity's conditioned insanity, because we have not been able to do so without correcting our perceptions or by using our past and current practices.

Part 2 of this book presents you with practices that grow out of the text of *The Leap*. Many of you are already using spiritual practices in your daily life. There is no suggestion that you drop these, but that you try to adopt at least a few of *The Leap* practices in order to put them to the test. Do these practices bring healing into your life? Because you have adopted them, are you a more peaceful, joyful, loving human being? I encourage you to try them all, then use whichever of them you are drawn to.

PRACTICE 1

Entering Stillness

You can intentionally enter stillness anywhere at any time. If this practice is new to you, it may be best to start with a daily practice of sitting
in stillness for 30 minutes shortly after you get up in the morning,
before the activities and responsibilities of the day are upon you. There
are two reasons for this. First, your mind will be less active at this hour
than later in the day. Second, you will take the benefits of your practice
of stillness into the rest of your day.

Choose a quiet place to sit in stillness. Sit upright, keeping your
body still, and close your eyes. Don't have any expectations of what is
supposed to happen. Simply hold the intention to enter the stillness
within you.

Let your breathing take you inward. Breathe naturally and simply
be conscious of your breath. Then notice the inhale stage and the exhale
stage. Next, intentionally make the exhale stage longer, and as you do,
feel yourself going deeper into the stillness. This can be achieved more
easily if, when you let go of the exhale, you also let go of any tension in
your body, allowing the body to deflate as it were. After you have done
this for three to five breathing cycles, go back to breathing naturally. At
this point, if you wish, you can take your attention off your breath and
simply be in the stillness.

If thoughts and feelings come, allow them to enter, then let them
go. If an insight or an impulse to do something emerges out of the stillness, make a mental note of it, then return your full attention to the

stillness. This also applies to any bodily sensations you may experience, including pain. Since most of us put little if any of our attention into our body, it often takes this opportunity to tell us where it hurts or where it is holding frozen energy from suppressed or repressed feelings that seek to be released. Whenever you feel soreness or a twinge of pain, bathe this area of your body with love and breathe into the place you feel the discomfort until it passes.

When you go within, you will become aware of an animating force that gives life to your whole body. In *The Power of Now,* Eckhart Tolle calls this our "inner body." The best way to remain anchored in stillness is to keep your attention on the sensations of your inner energy body.

If you are new to feeling your inner body, it may be difficult at first to feel the sensation of the energy to which I am referring. This is because we have been conditioned to give almost all of our attention to thoughts, emotions, and the external experiences of our everyday lives. Don't make an effort to feel your animating life force. If you are struggling to experience something, you can't be in stillness. Instead, be patient with yourself.

Since it is easier to feel your inner energy in the body's extremities than to feel it in your trunk, start by putting your attention on one hand, then the other. Now feel both hands at the same time. Next bring your attention to one foot, followed by the other. Now feel both feet at the same time. Then allow yourself to feel the energy in both hands and both feet at the same time.

Next, focus your attention on the whole of one upper limb, followed by the other. Now put your attention on both upper limbs together. Then switch your attention to the whole of one lower limb, then the other. Next, put your attention on both lower limbs simultaneously. From here, move to feeling the life within all four limbs at the same time.

Continue to bring your attention to other parts of your body until you can feel the whole of the energy body at once. The more you sit and practice feeling your inner body, the easier it will be to do so. The more intensely you feel the energy, the more sublime the experience.

With practice, you will carry this inner body energy with you beyond your isolated sitting practice into your daily activities. In other words, you will be aware of and participate in the external circumstances of your life, while simultaneously sensing the energy field of your inner Presence. When you are attuned to the energy of your inner Presence, you cannot become lost in the world of everyday events. On the contrary, you bring the healing and corrective power of Presence into all that you do and to all whom you meet.

PRACTICE 2

Quickly Accessing Inner Stillness During Challenging Times

You may be familiar with the particular practice of meditation that incorporates the silent repetition of a mantra or sacred word while sitting in stillness. A mantra's purpose is to facilitate the calming of your mind. It is a tool for centering yourself and entering into the state of *being*. One of the most powerful and familiar practices of this kind is to repeat the word *"om." Om* is the alpha and omega, and everything in between. It is the oneness, the "I Am." The verbal or silent saying of *om* and other sacred mantras carries a refined energy that cuts through the bone of our human nature and hits the marrow of our spiritual essence. It takes us "home."

In light of the leap we are making, I suggest augmenting this practice. People often refer to accessing their oneness with divine Self as "going home." We all long for this experience, although we often choose dysfunctional ways of trying to get home. I am suggesting that you use the very word "home" as a mantra, since it not only contains the sacred *om* but also helps evoke the feeling-state of being at home, which is characterized by feelings such as peace, safety and security, unconditional acceptance, a quiet joy, freedom, grace, and love. In other words, say this mantra with the intention of it taking you back to your state of felt oneness with your divine Self. You will be surprised how quickly it returns you to a state of *felt* realization of your being, especially at those times in life when you meet with a challenge.

If you cannot use the word "home" without it bringing up sadness or anxiety because of personal experiences, you may wish to avoid this particular practice. Alternatively, you could elect to redefine "home" in terms of a spiritual ideal.

Experiment with this mantra. Notice how it acts as a signal that it's time to go into your inner energy body, the field of Presence. As your attention shifts from your external world and into your inner reality, you enter a calm. You find yourself becoming centered. You can then bring this calm, centered state to your external circumstances.

If at first you find it hard to experience this state upon uttering "h-om-e," you can begin by silently saying "going h-om-e" until you start feeling you are at home in a spiritual sense. Then drop the word "going" and simply say "at h-om-e." Continue saying silently "at h-om-e" until you feel this blessed state of being. At this point, you can drop the word "at" and just say "h-om-e." Finally, when even the word "h-om-e" is a distraction, drop it too and rest in the still and silent arms of your own divine Presence.

Whenever you encounter anything that is disturbing, immediately say the word "h-om-e" silently to yourself. Enter into the calm of Presence and continue with your external activities from this state.

PRACTICE 3

Praying from Inner Stillness

In Practice 1, it was suggested that we not hold onto anything—thoughts, emotions, insights—when in stillness, but that we instead simply notice these, let them go, then put our attention back on our inner stillness by focusing on feeling again the energy of our inner body.

Sometimes, however, when sitting in stillness, you may feel an urge to pray for someone or some situation. If this happens, do not ignore it. This impulse is from stillness, so it is important for you to take it seriously. Stay in the inner body, but also incorporate the blessings and prayers that come to you from your heart center for that person or situation. Your prayer will be effective because it comes out of the still power of the universe within you.

~~~ PRACTICE 4

Stop Seeking Solutions Outside Yourself

Notice how pervasive seeking is in your life. What would it be like if you stopped seeking outside yourself for fulfillment, acceptance, guidance, or answers?

Ask yourself, "How would I feel if I stopped seeking outside myself?"

Go into stillness. Thirty seconds may suffice, or you may find yourself relishing the stillness for several minutes. Let your inner knower be the prompter for the length of time you spend in stillness. Revisit the question. Note the feelings that arise.

Now ask yourself, "How would my life change if I ceased seeking?"

Go into stillness. Revisit the question. Note the response that comes to you from stillness.

Finally, ask yourself, "What is preventing me from dropping the need to seek outside of myself right now?"

Go into stillness. Revisit the question. All you have to do at this point is become *aware* of the answer that comes to you. Awareness itself will take over from here.

PRACTICE 5

Drop Identification with the Body

Ask yourself, "What would happen if I no longer identified myself as a body?"

Go into stillness. Revisit the question. Note how your life would be different.

Next ask yourself, "What if I no longer identified others as being their body?"

Go into stillness. Revisit the question. Note how you would relate to others differently.

Finally, ask yourself, "What would happen to fear if I dropped identifying myself and others as bodies?"

Go into stillness. Revisit the question. Note the answer that comes to you.

PRACTICE 6

Drop Blaming, Judging, Scapegoating

Ask yourself, "What would life be like if I no longer judged or blamed others?"

Go into stillness. Revisit the question. Note your answer.

PRACTICE 7

Use Your Energy Wisely

When you catch yourself blaming, judging, or scapegoating, ask yourself, "How do I feel when I do this?"

Notice how you feel and assess your energy level when you blame, judge, or scapegoat.

When you catch yourself responding to a person or situation from a place of love, when you normally wouldn't, ask yourself, "How do I feel?"

Note how you feel and assess your energy level.

PRACTICE 8

For a Day, Observe How You Judge and Blame

Set aside one day to focus on observing how often you judge and blame. Pay attention as to who it is you treat this way and what situations evoke your judgment and blame.

At the end of the day, revisit your observations.

This can also be a daily practice.

PRACTICE 9

Set Aside a Day for Extending Your Light

Set aside one day in which you intentionally extend compassion, understanding, and acceptance to all.

At the end of the day, note how your day went, how you feel, and what your energy level was like throughout the day.

This can also be a daily practice.

PRACTICE 10

Become Aware That Your Finger Points Only at Yourself

Ask yourself, "What am I really doing when I judge, blame, or scapegoat?"

Don't try to answer the question, but simply go into stillness and allow understanding of your actions to arise from the stillness. Revisit the question. Note your answer.

Ask yourself, "When I blame, judge, scapegoat, what am *I* not taking responsibility for?"

Go into stillness. Revisit the question. Note your answer.

~~ PRACTICE 11

Look for the Good

Make a list of things you are not currently happy with in your life—people, situations, your own behavior.

Since your divine Self is present everywhere—in everyone and every situation—look for the good hidden in each item on your list and make note of it.

What are your overall conclusions after doing this practice?

The next time something "negative" happens to you and your impulse is to react to it, challenge yourself to look for the good in the situation then and there. Then smile!

PRACTICE 12

Drop Your Drama

Ask yourself, "Why do I enjoy drama so much—my own, and that of others?"

Go into stillness. Revisit the question. Note your answer.

Now ask yourself, "What would happen in my life if I dropped my infatuation with drama?"

Go into stillness. Revisit the question. Note your answer.

PRACTICE 13

Experience Your Divine Attributes

Make a complete list of the attributes you ascribe to God.

Since you cannot ascribe to another what you are not already, look at this list and tell yourself that in your divine Self, *you* are these things too. Note how you feel as you realize this about yourself.

Ask yourself, "Why is it so difficult for me to own my divine attributes?"

Go into stillness. Review the question. Note your answer.

Then ask yourself, "What would it be like if I *lived* my divine attributes in this moment right now—if I lived like the divine Self I am?"

Go into stillness. Review the question. Note your answer.

Finally, ask yourself, "What is preventing me from accepting my divine Self *now*?"

Go into stillness. Review the question. Note your answer.

PRACTICE 14

Extend Your Peace to Others

Set aside one full day to intentionally extend to others your divine attribute of peace by saying silently to those individuals you meet during your day, "Peace be with you."

At the end of the day, note how your day went and how you feel.

Make it an ongoing practice to extend peace to others in your life.

PRACTICE 15

Extend Your Love to Others

Set aside one full day to intentionally extend your divine attribute of love to those you meet during your day. Say silently to yourself when meeting someone, "How I love you!"

At the end of the day, note how your day went and how you feel.

Make it an ongoing practice to extend love to others in your life.

~~~~~~~~ PRACTICE 16

Extend Love Even When
You Find It Difficult

Set aside about half an hour when you can be alone and no one else can hear you. During this time, start thinking of people you love dearly. Now extend your sincere and deep love to each of them by saying out loud their name followed by, "I love you so!"

Once you have exhausted the list of those you hold closest to your heart, notice how you feel.

Now move on to a number of people you don't know well or feel quite neutral about. Extend your love to each of them, the same way you did with those you love dearly.

When you have finished with this group, pause and notice how you are feeling.

Finally, think of the people in your life who you feel you cannot love, and extend your love to these also, the same way you did with the former two groups. You may wish to start with those you feel only moderately negative about, then work up to those you just can't stand!

When you have finished with this group, notice how you feel.

When you can say to someone you think of as your enemy, "I love you so!"—and *mean* it—you know you will have made the Leap. There is tremendous redemptive power to be found in loving those we formerly hated. Why do you think this is so?

~~~ PRACTICE 17

Bless Others

As in Practice 16, say, using the person's name, "I bless you." Do this for each of the three categories of people mentioned, noting how you feel after blessing those in each category.

~~~ PRACTICE 18

Silently or Verbally Greet Others
in a Spiritual Manner

Some cultures already do this. For example, in India they say, "Namasté," when greeting another. In Hawaii they say, "Aloha," which means God in us. Jewish people greet others with, "Shalom," which means peace. In Arabic countries, they say, "As-Salamu Alaykum" ("Peace be upon you"). This is a constant reminder to them that when they meet another, the relationship is holy because each of the participants is holy. I muse that a day will soon come when all cultures have a word or phrase that accomplishes this same thing.

Ram Dass said, "Relationships are the dharma of the West." Extending a spiritual greeting to others is a way of reminding ourselves of this. Choose a sacred greeting that feels natural for you to extend to others, and do so either silently or verbally when you meet them.

PRACTICE 19

Take Your Blessings to the World

Set aside one day when you intentionally say silently to yourself, "I bless you," to all you encounter. Note how you feel at the end of the day. How were your relationships? How did your day go?

Make silently blessing others a regular practice.

PRACTICE 20

Bless Yourself

Sit in stillness for a minute or two. Then imagine what it would feel like to receive a blessing from someone.

Now, bless yourself, saying things like, "I bless my body. I bless my thoughts. I bless my beating heart. I bless my eyes."

Note how it feels to bless yourself. Make this an ongoing practice.

Take Inventory of the Attributes of Divine Love

Sit in stillness for a minute or two. Then take inventory of what divine love really means. What is it like? What are its qualities? Write down all of the attributes of divine love that come to mind. You may need to come back to this list a number of times to make additions until you feel it is complete.

Keep this list as a reminder of how you need to stretch your capacity for loving. You may want to emboss or frame your list to accord it special value and make it your very own.

What would it look like if you loved like your divine Self? Refer to your list at least once a day for a month and periodically thereafter, as you challenge yourself to a new level of loving.

PRACTICE 22

The Practice of Hooponopono

For the aspects of yourself that still require healing, you may wish to utilize the Hawaiian system of Hooponopono. In Hawaiian, hoo means "cause" and ponopono means "perfection." Hooponopono can be used to heal your wounds through a process of repentance and forgiveness.

Each of us brings into our daily life years of toxic patterns of thought and emotion that reside in the unconscious. These may have accumulated from all the way back through our many generations of ancestors. When this toxicity occupies the unconscious, it manifests as negative conditions in our everyday lives. We then draw to us people, events, and situations that reflect these unconscious states that need healing.

Whenever we encounter anything that causes us not to be at peace, this is a signal that we are not yet experiencing our divine Self in this aspect of our lives. Hooponopono is a way to get in touch with the divinity that is our true being. By ridding ourselves of our negative unconscious states, we access our divine center, which is the gateway to complete freedom from anything negative in our past or present.

If you experience anything in someone else that troubles you, such as anger, self-pity, or some other negative emotion, this points to something that still needs healing in your own life. Instead of blaming the other person, take 100% responsibility for your reaction. If you are reacting in any way, you or your ancestors have at some time and in some way contributed to creating the inner state you are now experiencing.

In Hooponopono, taking responsibility in this way is called "repentance," which means to think afresh. To repent enables us to see ourselves in an entirely new light, as we truly are in our divinity. Repentance brings about forgiveness. Seeing ourselves differently, we can forgive ourselves for all of the negativity we have created and clear it from our unconscious.

Part of the process of experiencing forgiveness is to express our love for the person or situation that causes or has caused us upset. It is helpful to thank the person or situation for being in our lives, if not in person at least in our heart, since they came into our life to cause us grief only because we invited them at a deep unconscious level. Their purpose was to present us with an opportunity to heal some wounded aspect of our psyche. When we recognize this and respond with forgiveness and gratitude, the divine within us flows like a healing balm, transmuting our suffering into peace. Forgiveness is redemptive—healing and transforming—because we flood those aspects of our lives in which we have not yet experienced our divinity with the love that always comes as awareness dawns. As our psyche is restored to wholeness, we heal our external world as well.

Let me illustrate how this works in everyday life. If someone comes into your life who has just had a divorce and this generates a negative response in you, ask yourself what in you needs healing. What is it about you that is reflected in your reaction to this person getting a divorce? Take 100% responsibility for healing this in yourself by going through the steps of saying to yourself regarding this person, "I'm sorry. Forgive me. I love you. Thank you."

The same applies if you have an intense dislike of someone, or your family is demonstrating a lot of uncaring behavior towards one another, or you are a psychologist and your client is suffering from depression.

When you experience anything that is not based in peace and love—including matters of a collective nature—continue to say this releasing and healing sequence of short sentences. Sometimes you may need to say the sequence multiple times before the negative unconscious memory within you is released. You will know it has been released when the same situation in your external world no longer upsets you, and you instead find yourself feeling neutral, or feeling acceptance, peace, and love for the person or situation—or the condition simply disappears.

This Hawaiian practice of repentance, forgiveness, and transmutation can be an ongoing practice. As already stated, the practice consists of saying to yourself in silence, or out loud if you are alone, the following short sentences in the sequence given:

Forgive me.

When I see some person or situation in the world to which I react (that is, do not respond with peace and acceptance), it is a sign that this situation or person is mirroring to me an aspect of myself that I have not yet healed within myself. Saying, "Forgive me," is accepting responsibility for what I, or my ancestors, have created or contributed to creating in my world. It is the first step to self-healing.

I am sorry.

This statement is an admission that I want healing.

I love you.

Silently expressing this to the person or situation brings in the transformative power of love to heal what still needs healing in myself that is being mirrored to me.

Thank you.

I thank the person or situation for showing up in my life right now to remind me that there are still places that I need to heal within myself and for prompting me to do so.

Whenever you react to anything negative in your world, it is a reminder that there is still something that needs healing in *you*. So when you are upset by addiction in a loved one, rage in your boss at work, or selfishness in your sibling, you have a wonderful opportunity to heal yourself. Since we are all one, as you heal yourself, the other person or situation is healed in some measure as well.

PRACTICE 23

Be the Things You Want to See in Others

You can intentionally elect to *be* the things you want to see in others.

If you want to see peace, bring peace into all your thoughts and everything you do. If you want others to be loving, bring love into all of your relationships. If you want people to accept others regardless of physical, social, religious, and other differences, *be* unconditionally accepting of all.

If we do not practice what we preach—*before* we preach it—our preaching will be empty and ineffective. It is only when we embody the characteristics we want to see practiced wholesale in our world that we have the power to bring them about.

The reason Jesus the Christ, Mahatma Gandhi, Mother Teresa, and all effective spiritual teachers have such a positive influence on others is because they embody their teachings. Their lives have integrity because what they say is matched by what they do.

PRACTICE 24

Set Noble Intentions

In Part I, a distinction was made between fear-driven, ego-based intentions, and heart-based noble intentions. We saw that we cannot just
pluck a noble intention out of the air—that it has to emerge sincerely
from the heart. Once we set a noble intention, we let it go at the mind
level, but we continue to hold it in our heart.

Invite noble intentions to come to the fore in your life over the next
two weeks. List them as they come to you. Refer to this list for at least
six months to see how these intentions become manifest.

PRACTICE 25

Set a Daily Intention

Make it a regular practice to set a noble intention for the day shortly after you awaken in the morning.

PRACTICE 26

Join in Noble Intent

Refer to the list you made in Practice 24. Some of these intentions easily lend themselves to inviting another or others to join you in them. If potential participants are not obvious, seek out someone to join you in at least one of these intentions.

Keep in mind that joining together in noble intent has to be sincere. The intention must be truly owned by all parties.

Refer to your list of conjoint intentions over the next six months to see how they become manifest.

PRACTICE 27

Pray with Noble Intent

We are shifting from praying to outside forces, including our perceptions of a God who is separate from us, to prayers of intent. Praying to a power outside of us fosters a sense of helplessness, whereas prayers of intent foster a sense of empowerment as we accept our role as co-creators of our universe.

A Buddhist prayer called the Meta Prayer of Loving Kindness may serve us well in making the shift we seek to make. The prayer is as follows:

May I be at peace.
May my heart remain open.
May I awaken to the light of my own true nature.
May I be healed.
May I be a source of healing for all beings.

You can see how this prayer can be said as a request. But it can also be said with noble intent. I suggest that you say it once as a request, then say it again as an intention. Notice the difference in where the energy is focused in your body when you say the prayer as a request, compared with when you say it with intention.

Now substitute "may you" for "may I" in the prayer. Say it as a request, then as an intention, and again note the different feeling you have from each.

Finally, substitute "may we" for "may you." This time say it only as an intention. Start by imagining "we" as a small group, such as your family or your team of co-workers. Then say the prayer several more times, each time expanding the size of the group until "we" becomes the entire galaxy.

PRACTICE 28

Note Evidence of Oneness in Your Life

What experiences have you either had yourself, or read about, that indicate that we are not separate from each other but are truly one? Note these.

Now keep your eyes and ears open for further evidence of oneness during the next two weeks. As incidents of this kind occur, add these to your list. You can keep this as an open list and continue to look for evidence that we are all one.

When we actively look for such evidence, life steps up at the other end to bring it to us.

~~~ PRACTICE 29

Invite Someone to Join You in Presence

When you are planning to meet someone, especially for the first time, before you do so, invite the Presence in that person to join with the Presence in you. This will have a tremendous effect on how you relate when you meet.

You may also want to imagine a string going from your heart to the other person's. Tug on the string from your heart, thereby issuing an invitation for the person to join you at the heart level when you meet.

Note how you feel toward the other person when you get together. Note how the person relates to you.

~~~ PRACTICE 30

Listen from Presence

When you listen to someone who is caught up in their drama, intentionally go into stillness. Listen to the person from a state of Presence.

Pay little attention to the content of what the person is talking about, placing 90% of your attention on the divine Self that is the essence of the individual behind the story. Notice how differently you relate to the person when you are relating from Presence. Notice also how the other person begins to relate differently to you and to their drama.

PRACTICE 31

Pray with the Angels, Saints, and Ascended Masters

Jesus taught his disciples to pray in his name. For most, this has become a rote tacking on of the phrase, "In Jesus' name, amen," at the end of their requests. Jesus had in mind something quite different from such a mechanical practice.

Since our oneness with everything includes those beings who have gone beyond the physical body—who have ascended—we can call them to join with us in our intentions when we pray. Jesus is one such person.

Since intentions each carry their own characteristic energy, we will naturally call in those who have ascended with whom we have a special closeness, or those whose energy signatures will be helpful in addressing our specific intent. How powerful prayer then becomes!

We may say something like, "Dearest Archangel Michael, Master Jesus, Master St. Germaine, my guides and guardian angels, and all of my unseen helpers, I invite you to join me now in our oneness and with the intent that (specify the intent)." We then go into stillness for a minute, while holding to the energy of our intent, knowing that those we invoked are one with us in this intent. It is appropriate to end by blessing and thanking those we have invoked in oneness.

When praying for others, it can be helpful to call in those aspects of our oneness that are especially meaningful to the person for whom we are praying. In such a case, our prayer may go something like, "Kuan Yin, Archangel Raphael, my loved one's guides, her guardian angels, and all of her unseen helpers, I invite you to join me in the intent that (state the person's name for whom you are praying and your loving intent for them)."

Go into stillness for a minute, while holding to the energy of your intent, knowing that those you have invoked are holding to this intent with you. End by blessing and thanking those you have invoked from oneness.

PRACTICE 32

When You Don't Know How
To Pray for Someone

Often we are concerned about our loved ones but don't really know what is best for them. Consequently, we are at a loss about how to pray for them. For example, if a person is very aged, should we pray that they be physically healed, or that they find the grace to leave the body peacefully?

At such times, it is a relief to know that we don't have to be clear on what is best for the person we care about. We can turn the praying over to our inner knower, the omniscience of our divine Self.

In such a situation, our prayer may go something like this, "Inner knower, I don't know how to pray for _____, so I ask you to pray in the silence and stillness the perfect prayer for them." Then simply rest in the stillness, knowing that your inner knower is praying and that its prayer will be for the highest and best for your loved one and all concerned.

PRACTICE 33

Affirm the I Am Presence

I Am is another term for divine Source or God.

Affirm the I Am Presence when you are worried about someone or some situation. For example, your troubled teenager or the current war in Iraq. Knowing that the I Am Presence is all there is, and that it is universally present everywhere at all times, as well as beyond time, you can say in confidence, "I Am here, and the I Am is there, as my son. I Am here, and the I Am is there in Iraq. I Am peace and harmony. Peace and harmony are with my son and in Iraq."

Indeed, when you want to demonstrate strength or any other of your divine attributes, affirm that the I Am is the only Presence acting in you. Or whenever you wish someone well when things seem to be going wrong, affirm that I Am is the only presence acting within that individual. If the person needs healing of their body, for example, you can affirm that the I Am is the only Presence in that body.

~~~ PRACTICE 34

Experience Oneness through the Practice of Gazing

For this practice you will need a willing partner. Gazing takes place between two individuals who mutually agree that they want to gaze into each other's eyes for the purpose of seeing through the physical eyes to the Presence within each other.

The power of this practice is that, by seeing the Presence within another, you become acutely aware of your own Presence. This also awakens realization of your oneness with the person.

Gazing can last a few seconds or several minutes. The length of time is determined intuitively by the gazers.

⁓ PRACTICE 35

From Affirmative to Confirmative Prayer

Affirmative prayer is not the kind of prayer in which we make a request. Affirmative prayer involves making positive statements about what we intend to experience. When we pray affirmatively, we pray as if something we intend is already so, and through affirmation call it into manifestation.

For example, if you are out of work, an affirmative prayer would be, "I am working at the perfect job for me." Similarly, if you are experiencing ill health, you might affirm, "I am experiencing robust health and optimal vitality." Your affirmations may also be more encompassing, such as, "The world is a safe place to be. Abundance flows to all people on the planet. I know that I am divine, and now demonstrate all of the attributes of my divine Self."

It is a leap to go from prayers of request, which often have a note of desperation to them—and often become rote, as if repetition somehow intensifies their effectiveness—to affirmative prayer. You may find yourself thinking, "What foolishness to declare I have something that I don't actually have. I'm not playing those mind games. Isn't it for God to give me such things if I am deserving?"

Affirmative prayer uses the mind as a springboard. In affirmative prayer, we affirm something as if it were already so, when there is no sensory or experiential evidence that it is. We put all of our mental muscle behind our affirmation and never waiver, never doubt. Affirmative prayer recognizes our oneness with God. It is based on our faith in our power to co-create.

Refer back to Practice 13 in which you made a list of divine attributes. Now appropriate and affirm these attributes, preferably out loud. To hear yourself making such affirmations may sound outrageous at first—certainly beyond any possibility of living this way. This is because you are breaking through thousands of years of egoic conditioning in order to awaken your true self. Remember that a leap means leaving one place and moving into totally different territory, so such affirmations are bound to feel odd at first.

The next challenge is to take still another leap—an even bigger one—and go from affirmative prayer to confirmative prayer. Confirmative statements emerge from Presence. They are statements of direct *knowing* that come out of inner stillness and direct experience.

Confirmative prayer is not wishful thinking or hoping. It is *entrusting ourselves to what we know.*

How do we take the leap from affirmative to confirmative prayer?

Confirmative prayer is not possible without cultivating present moment awareness and inner stillness.

In confirmative prayer, we go beyond affirmative prayer and personally *extend* our divine attributes to our world by the way we live. As we experience a fullness of love, joy, and peace, we find ourselves being prompted to share these with others. We don't seek peace, we *are* peace. We don't seek love, we *are* love. We don't seek good things, we *are* a source of all good things.

As we continue to give from our divine Self, we will experience how wonderful it feels to live this way, and we will continue to do so until we live and move and have our *be*-ing in our divine Self. We know we have made the Leap when we say, "I Am love, and peace, and joy," and this is no longer a matter of affirmation, but of confirmation of what we really *know.*

An amazing thing happens when we live this way. We find that everything we give, we give to ourselves. In other words, we receive back what we put out. And because our divine Self doesn't know how to give merely in equal measure, every good thing we give out comes back to us multiplied. Our life *overflows* with the attributes of divinity.

Anyone who has come to realize their divine Self uses confirmative language when they speak. This is why the words of Jesus the Christ, the Buddha, and all true spiritual teachers have such power.

PRACTICE 36

A Leap Prayer

Here is a prayer that we can use both to facilitate us in making the Leap and also to measure our progress in doing so. It is to be seen as only one part of *The Leap* Practices.

I have come to know the divine Self I Am
I serve from the light of my inner Presence
I experience my oneness with all that is
I love with the divine love that I Am
I live the reality of my divine Self by *be*-ing it in my world

I invite you to say this prayer daily. At first you will be affirming what you don't yet experience. Continue your Leap Practices and continue to say this prayer until these are confirmative statements, expressing what you truly know to be so.

Part II—Conclusion

F YOU HAVE READ this far, my gratitude for having
given *The Leap* a full hearing.

The practices presented in Part II are to assist you in
establishing a new spiritual practice or augmenting an existing one. As
you continue in your Leap practices, you will likely experience wanting
to modify them to better suit your own inclinations. Also, you may be
moved to establish new personal Leap practices. This is an indicator
that you are opening to your own inner knower, which speaks to you
out of stillness and is ever creative.

It is truly wonderful that we are alive on the planet at this time—a
time in the evolution of humanity that calls for the Leap and for the first
time also makes it possible. We are in this together, each of us learning
as we move forward just what the Leap really entails. May we share and
learn from one another in this endeavor, and may we always remember
that we have companions with us as we step up to this challenge.

Namasté.

NOTES

1   Broadcast to the United States by General Douglas MacArthur, from the Battleship Missouri in Tokyo Bay, September 2, 1945, after the surrender ceremonies that officially concluded World War II.

2   Jn. 8:7.

3   Beschloss, Michael, *Presidential Courage: Brave Leaders and How They Changed America 1789-1989* (New York, London, Sydney: Simon & Schuster, 2007), pp. 296-324.

4   Prov. 29:18.

5   McMoneagle, Joseph, *Memoirs of a Psychic Spy. The Remarkable Life of U.S. Government Remote Viewer 001* (Hampton Roads, Charlottesville, VA, 2006), p. 45.

6   Jn. 10:10.

7   *A Course in Miracles* (Foundation of Inner Peace, Glen Allen, California, 1990), Text, Ch. 12, p. 210.

8   Matt. 5:48.

9   *A Course in Miracles*, Text, Ch. 6, p. 87.

10   Lk. 23:46.

11   *A Course in Miracles*, Text, Introduction.

12   Matt. 6:20.

13 Jn. 10:31.

14 *A Course in Miracles*, Manual for Teachers, Clarification of Terms, p. 73.

15 Lk. 6:38.

16 I Chron. 4:10.

17 Gen. 1:3.

18 *A Course in Miracles*, Text, Ch. 7, p. 104.

19 *Ibid.* While *A Course in Miracles* uses the male gender language, it refers to all of humanity.

20 Matt. 18:20.

21 Acts 2:1.

22 Ibn Arabi, born in 1165, an Arab Muslim mystic and philosopher.

23 For a description of this, see *The Great Story: Death of the Dinosaurs*, Connie Barlow, www.thegreatstory.org/dinosaurs.

24 Whitman, Walt, "Leaves of Grass," 1990.

25 *A Course in Miracles*, Text, Ch. 5, p. 82.

26 *A Course in Miracles,* Text, Ch. 26, p. 522.

27 Brown, Michael, *The Presence Process: A Healing Journey into Present Moment Awareness* (Vancouver, Canada, and New York, NY: Namaste Publishing and Beaufort Books, 2005), p. 232.

28 Matt. 28:18.

n

NAMASTE PUBLISHING

Our Publishing Mission is to make available healing and
transformational publications that acknowledge, celebrate, and
encourage readers to live from their true essence and thereby come to
remember Who They Really Are.

*

Namaste Publishing
P.O. Box 62084
Vancouver, British Columbia V6J 4A3
Canada
www.namastepublishing.com
Email: namaste@telus.net
Tel: 604-224-3179
Fax: 604-224-3354

To place an order, see www.namastepublishing.com, or
Email: namasteproductions@shaw.ca

To schedule Constance Kellough for a teaching or speaking event,
Email: namasteteachings@telus.net

To receive the full benefit of books from Namaste Publishing, we
invite you to read our daily blog: "He said … She said …"

We also invite you to sign up for our free Email Newsletter, in which
we bring you articles by our staff writers, book and movie reviews,
frequent free downloads from our authors, and information about
forthcoming publications.

You may sign up for both the BLOG and the NEWSLETTER by
going to our home page: www.namastepublishing.com